T0208507

VERSO
CLASSICS

The last few decades have seen an immense outpouring of works of theory and criticism, but, as the number of titles has increased dramatically, it has become more and more difficult to find one's way around this vast body of literature and to distinguish between those works of real and enduring value and those of a more ephemeral nature. The Verso Classics series will rise to the challenge by taking stock of the last few decades of contemporary critical thought and reissuing, in an elegant paperback format and at affordable prices, those books which genuinely constitute original and important intellectual contributions.

Many of these works are currently out of print or difficult to obtain: Verso Classics will bring them back into the public domain, building a collection which will become the 'essential left library'.

The Ideology of
Power and the
Power of Ideology

GÖRAN THERBORN

VERSO

London · New York

© Göran Therborn, 1980
First published by Verso 1980
All rights reserved

Second impression 1982
Third impression 1988
Fourth impression (Verso Classics edition) 1999

Verso
UK: 6 Meard Street, London W1V 3HR
USA: 180 Varick Street, New York NY 10014-4606

Verso is the imprint of New Left Books

ISBN 978-1-85984-212-6

Filmset in Compset Times by
Villiers Publications, London

Printed in Great Britain by
Biddles Ltd, Guildford and King's Lynn

Contents

Preface

What follows here is an essay — marked by all the tentativeness, modesty and limitation this word connotes — on a range of topics that really require a full-scale treatise, or several. It is published as a book for the reason that, while the text turned out much too long for the article it set out to be, I continued to believe that there were serious deficiencies in current studies and discussions of ideology which called for an intervention, however preliminary and lapidary.

My dissatisfaction with predominant tendencies in the field centres on four problem-areas. First, there is a need to argue for the *dialectical* character of ideology, a dialectic indicated by the two opposite senses of the word 'subject' ('the subjects of history'/'the subjects of the prince'). Ideologies not only subject people to a given order. They also qualify them for conscious social action, including actions of gradual or revolutionary change. Ideologies do not function merely as 'social cement'.

Second, it seems more accurate and fruitful to see ideologies, not as possessions, as ideas possessed, but as *social processes*. That is, to see them as complex social processes of 'interpellation' or address, speaking to us. In these continuous processes ideologies overlap, compete and clash, drown or reinforce each other. The actual operation of ideology in contemporary society is better illustrated by the cacophony of sounds and signs of a big city street than by the text serenely communicating with the solitary reader, or the teacher or TV-personality addressing a quiet, domesticated audience.

Third, I think the questions raised by Marx about the *material determination* of ideologies should be confronted explicitly, and not (as contemporary Marxists have tended to prefer), bypassed in embarrassed silence, or simply repeated, interpreted and re-interpreted in an endless series of Marxological exegeses. What is attempted here is a new formulation of a theory of material determination and of class ideologies.

Finally, it seems to me that the usual treatment of ideology in *political* theory and analysis is unsatisfactory. With this in mind, I discuss such conceptions as the force/consent dichotomy, legitimacy, consensus and revolutionary class consciousness as crucial preconditions of and factors in revolutionary change, submitting them to critical scrutiny in the context of the main theses presented here.

These critical concerns are, of course, by no means unique to this essay, which builds upon path-breaking contributions already made, and it is my intention and hope that it will connect with ongoing reflections, research and debates, some divergent, others parallel, still others convergent.

Before committing his text to the judgment of the reader, an author has to thank all who have helped him. In this case they are very numerous and my debt of gratitude to them great. I have benefited enormously from a large number of detailed, constructive criticisms made by Perry Anderson, Francis Mulhern, Gunnar Olofsson and Erik Olin Wright. I have also received very valuable comments from Anthony Barnett, Robin Blackburn, Terry Freiberg, from the members of my seminar on ideology at the Boston University Summer School in 1978, and from the participants in the extraordinarily stimulating workshop on 'Authority in Industrial Societies' organized by the European Consortium for Political Research and the Canadian Political Science Association in Brussels in April 1979. Kjel Törnblom has given me some very valuable bibliographical help. Patrick Camiller has taken great pains to make my English printable. Many thanks to all of you.

Göran Therborn,
Göteborg, April 1980

Introduction

Demarcations and Departures

The main concern of this essay is the operation of ideology in the organization, maintenance, and transformation of power in society. From the point of view of a class analysis of social domination, this involves questions about the role of ideology in class rule and class struggle. My aims are basically theoretical in character: to develop some analytical concepts and explanatory propositions about the operation of ideology in power relationships and social change. In a sense, what is presented here is a sequel to *What Does the Ruling Class Do When It Rules?*[1] — a work that was also concerned with the organization, reproduction and transformation of power, but whose central focus was the state.

These concerns and intentions themselves delimit to some extent my consideration of the almost inexhaustible topic, 'ideology'. But there remain many possible entries to, and paths through, the field of ideology; to give the reader a fair chance to evaluate the particular one taken here, some rationale for it is required at the outset. Above all, there is a need for some rudimentary but motivated definitions of what will be discussed; and the present text should be explicitly situated in a conjuncture of theory and research, in relation to whose questions and problems it is written.

'*Ideology*' will be used here in a very broad sense. It will not necessarily imply any particular content (falseness, miscognition, imaginary as opposed to real character), nor will it assume any necessary degree of elaboration and coherence. Rather it will refer to that aspect of the human condition under which human beings live their lives as conscious actors in a world that makes sense to them to varying degrees. Ideology is the medium through which this consciousness and meaningfulness operate. The consciousness of every new-born human being is formed through largely unconscious psychodynamic processes, and it functions in and through a symbolic order of language codes. Ideology, however, is not reducible to either of these.

Thus the conception of ideology employed here deliberately includes both everyday notions and 'experience' and elaborate intellectual doctrines, both the 'consciousness' of social actors and the institutionalized thought-systems and discourses of a given society. But to study these as ideology means to look at them from a particular perspective: not as bodies of thought or structures of discourse *per se*, but as manifestations of a particular being-in-the-world of conscious actors, of human subjects. In other words, to conceive of a text or an utterance as ideology is to focus on the way it operates in the formation and transformation of human subjectivity.

From this perspective a distinction may be drawn between, on the one hand, ideology, and, on the other, science, art, philosophy and law. This distinction pertains primarily to different dimensions of analysis, and only secondarily to intrinsic content. Not all ideology is or can operate as science, art, philosophy, or law, but all these emerge out of ideological configurations and may function as ideologies. Like all human activities, scientific, aesthetic, philosophical and legal practices are always enmeshed in ideology, but their emergence as specific, institutionalized practices in a historical division of labour also involves a 'break' or 'rupture' with surrounding ideologies through the production of specific discourses geared to producing special effects, separate from everyday experience and persuasion.

In the case of science this break meant the discovery-production of patterns of determination and systematic investigation of their operation.[2] However, the constitution of a particular discourse called science means neither that its practice is or will remain immune from the subjectivity of its practitioners, nor that it is incapable of affecting the subjectivity of the members of society, of functioning as ideology. The works of Adam Smith, Marx and Darwin, for instance, constitute works of science and can be studied, evaluated, developed, attacked or defended, as such. But they have also operated as ideologies, as 'economic liberalism', 'scientific socialism' and 'Social Darwinism', and may also be studied, evaluated, developed or resisted, in these senses, in terms of their diffusion, efficacy, and implications.

This essay is not an endeavour of Marxological exegesis, but since I consider myself to work on the basis of historical materialism, a brief clarification of the relationship of my conception of ideology to that of Marx is called for. In Marx we may discern at least two different conceptions of ideology or the ideological. One of them is basically the same as that adopted here. Ideology is then seen as the medium through which men make their history as conscious actors. In this sense, it refers to the 'forms in which men become conscious of this conflict [between the forces and the relations of production] and fight it out'. Within this perspective there are two basic concerns. One inquires how given ideologies are to be explained and involves the problems of material determination. The other has to do with the struggle between different class ideologies and their relationship to non-class ideologies. The former is dealt with by Marx and Engels in brief theoretical statements, the latter above all in letters of political advice to the labour movement.[3] It is this path, and these concerns, that I follow here.

However, this perception of ideology is linked to and dominated by another, in the works of Marx and Engels. Here 'ideology' refers to a false, idealist approach to and understanding of human consciousness and the motives of human action. 'Ideology is a process accomplished by the so-called thinker consciously, it is true, but with a false consciousness. The real forces impelling him remain unknown to him; otherwise it simply would not be an ideological process.... He works with mere thought material, which he accepts without examination as the product of thought, and does not investigate further for a more remote source independent of thought'.[4] Here the opposition is not between bourgeois and proletarian ideology, but between science and ideology as such, true and false consciousness.

It is this latter conception of ideology that has become dominant in the Marxist tradition, and echoes still in Althusser. I have broken with it here because it has been tied to a view of human motivation that I find untenable. This view of motivation held the two conceptions of ideology together in the works of Marx and Engels. Basically, they tended to regard the 'superstructure' of forms of consciousness as epiphenomena. Human behaviour was determined by 'interest', by class interests. The forms of consciousness either corresponded to these 'interests', as 'true' consciousness, or not, in which case they were illusions, and as such ineffective (at least in the longer run). This alternative is exemplified in Marx's treatment both of bourgeois ideology,[5] and of proletarian ideology, the latter in the form of a firm belief that the working class would develop a true consciousness of its class interests, in spite of the distorting appearances of capitalist relations of production, in spite of 'reification', 'commodity fetishism' and the 'wage-form' of exploitation.

This notion of motivation by interest assumes that normative conceptions of what is good and bad and conceptions of what is possible and impossible are given in the reality of existence and are accessible only through true knowledge of the latter.[6] In my opinion these are unwarranted and untenable assumptions. They represent a utilitarian residue in Marxism, which should be rejected, explicitly and decisively, once for all.

The broad definition of ideology adopted here departs from the usual Marxist one, by not restricting it to forms of illusion and miscognition, and also from the usual liberal conception, which is not accepted mainly because I think we should refuse to take what it implies for granted — that forms of consciousness and meaning that are not set out in more or less coherent doctrines are either unimportant in the organization of, and struggles for, power, or are self-evident, pragmatic 'common sense' (as in the notorious 'end of ideology' thesis).

Finally, it should be noted that, for all its breadth, this definition of ideology does retain a specific analytical dimension, which makes it distinguishable from, say, political structures or processes, economic relations, or forces of production. In this respect it differs from the almost all-inclusive notion of 'culture' deployed in much British writing on working-class culture,[7] and from François Châtelet's equally inclusive definition of ideology, which covers nearly everything between the 'long duration' of linguistic structures and the 'short duration' of events, such as 'structures of kinship, techniques of survival (and development)', 'the organization of power'.[8] These all-embracing definitions tend either to conceal the fact that a much narrower definition is actually being employed, or, if taken seriously, to drown everything in the same water.

Raymond Williams, whose great work on culture no student of ideology can afford to ignore, has rightly criticized the idea that 'base' and 'superstructure' are 'separable concrete entities'.[9] What he has made less clear and emphatic, however, is the equally important point that 'indissoluble real processes' may in their actual operation have diverse, analytically distinguishable dimensions, and that an adequate grasp of the former may precisely require these clear analytical distinctions. Even apart from the fact that 'culture' operates as an important figure of discourse, the study of which is fascinating in itself (as in Williams's own *Culture and Society*), the concept of culture may be useful alongside a broad definition of ideology. It may, for instance, be employed either as a shorthand for the ensemble of everyday activities and ideologies of a particular group or class, or as a more general, inclusive concept for ideology, science and art and, possibly, other practices studied from the point of view of their production of meaning.

However, the concept of ideology is not dependent on a concept of culture, contrary to what has recently been argued by Richard Johnson. His position is that 'ideologies never address ("interpellate") a "naked" subject'. And: 'ideologies always work upon a ground: that ground is *culture*'. But the theoretical redundancy of the concept becomes clear when we substitute one of Johnson's own two definitions of 'culture' for the word itself: 'ideologies always work upon a ground': that ground is 'the complex of ideologies that are actually adopted as moral preferences or principles of life'.[10] Althusser said something similar ten years ago: 'ideology has always-already interpellated individuals as subjects'.[11]

Classes are here defined strictly in economic terms, denoting the 'bearers' or 'agents' of particular relations of production. This is in accordance with the classical Marxist tradition but differs from the usage of Nicos Poulantzas, who insists that classes must be defined at the political and ideological, as well as the economic, 'level'. To *define* classes in ideological terms, however, precludes one of the most problematic questions that a materialist theory of ideology must confront: how are ideologies and classes of economic agents related?

'*Power*' will in this context refer mainly to political power in the usual sense, to the centralized condensation of social power-relationships invested in the state. This is, above all, simply a choice of analytical interest on my part. But in view of the current vogue for Foucault's 'micropolitics' of power, the crucial significance of the state for all societal relations of power should perhaps be underlined.[12]

This essay is situated in a particular theoretical conjuncture — a conjuncture of Marxist discourse on ideology opened by Althusser and his essay 'Ideology and Ideological State Apparatuses'. While the most widespread effect of this essay may have been to make fashionable the rather dubious notion of 'ideological state apparatuses' as a handy institutional label, its real, twofold importance lay elsewhere. First, Althusser conceptualized, explicitly and clearly, the operation of ideology in terms of the formation of human subjectivity, thus linking Marxist social theory to psychodynamics and psychoanalysis. Second, he broke with the tradition of viewing ideology as a body of ideas or thought, conceiving it instead as a social process of address, or 'interpellations', inscribed in material social matrices.

These contributions provide the starting-point of the present essay. If it begins *from* them, rather than simply applying Althusser's theory to new areas, this is because they are, in some important respects, still confined within limits from which a developed theory of ideology will have to break free. Althusser's work on ideology has stimulated a lively discussion, in which a number of questions have been raised or implicitly introduced. The concepts and propositions set out below are my own contribution, but there is no space here for any detailed comments on the discussion so far, or on other recent works on ideology.[13]

To me there seem to be two main flaws in Althusser's conception of ideology. First, there is the problem of what we shall call the mode of ideological interpellation, that is to say, what ideologies tell the subjects they address and constitute. In Althusser's view ideology represents an 'imaginary distortion of the real relations' of individuals to the relations of production, and to the relations that derive from them. This definition is related to two theses, both of which I find untenable: 1. that only scientific knowledge is 'true' or 'real' knowledge, all other forms of cognition (in everyday experience, for example) being distortions or forms of miscognition; 2. that human beings are (significantly) motivated as subjects only by what they know, by true or distorted knowledge. The first of these theses I have rejected in my definition of ideology. But the break with it must also entail a new conception of the material matrix within which the domination of a given ideology is reproduced — a conception that provides room for the (re)production of non-scientific experience and learning. A break with the second thesis requires the development of a conception of different modes of ideological interpellation in the constitution of motivated subjects.

Second, there is the question of the relationship of class to ideology, which was not explicitly raised and still less answered by Althusser. He did posit that the 'ideological state apparatuses' are both a stake and a site of the class struggle, and that the ideology of the ruling class is realized through the class struggle in them. But this is at once too little and too much. Too little in that it neither defends nor transcends the classical Marxist problematic centred on the material, class determination of ideologies. Too much because it takes as transparent the notions of class ideology (Althusser is mainly referring to ruling-class ideology) and ruling-class ideological domination.

There is a hiatus in Althusser's argument which seems to be determined, not through logical necessity but as a close contingent possibility, by the essential problematic of his text: the mechanisms of reproduction of a given mode of production. On the one hand, Althusser talks of class relations of exploitation, which have to be reproduced, and class struggle, through the mechanisms of which reproduction is asserted. On the other, he discusses individuals, the formation of their subjectivity and of their submission to the given social order. However, he omits the question of how classes are constituted as struggling forces, resisting exploitation or actively engaged in it.

In drawing a line of demarcation from stratification concepts of class, contemporary Marxists, particularly in the Althusserian tradition, have laid great stress on the idea that 'classes exist only in a relation of class struggle'. But this is only a definition, which does not answer the question: how are classes constituted as human forces in struggle? It should be clear, though to many writers it apparently is not,[14] that 'struggle' does not follow logically from the concept of relations of production, from the definition of classes as occupying the places of producers and appropriators of surplus labour. 'Exploitation' does not *per se* imply *resistance* to exploitation, the exploiters' resistance to the resistance of the exploited, or a struggle over exploitation as such. Despite the pejorative connotations of the word, the concept of 'exploitation' in historical materialism refers simply to the separate appropriation of surplus labour; in other words, to the fact that one category of economic agents works more than is necessary for their own reproduction and that the fruits of their surplus labour are appropriated by another. Instead of trying to confront the problem of the ideological constitution of struggling class subjects, many Marxists have tended to fall back on the crude utilitarian notion of 'interest': it is in the 'interest' of the exploited to resist exploitation and of the exploiters to defend it. But 'interests' by themselves do not *explain* anything. 'Interest' is a *normative* concept indicating the most rational course of action in a predefined game, that is, in a situation in which gain and loss have already been defined. The problem to be explained, however, is how members of different classes come to define the world and their situation and possibilities in it in a particular way. The attempt to confront systematically the problems of ideology and class also requires clarification of the relationship between class ideology and subjectivity, and possible forms of human subjectivity other than those of class membership.

These criticisms of Althusser amount to saying that the further development of a theory of ideology requires a shift or broadening of the object of inquiry from the role of ideology in the reproduction of exploitation and power to the generation, reproduction, and transformation of ideologies. It requires, then, a break from the lingering restrictions of Althusser's problematic of the sixties, most notably the rigid demarcation between science and ideology. And on this basis it is possible to return to the questions raised by Althusser, and to offer more nearly adequate answers.

Finally, with all due respect to Althusser, a discussion of ideology and power cannot confine itself to his formulation of the task: to examine the reproduction of exploitative relations of production, and the problems this raises. Just as pertinent is the Gramscian problematic of historical social formations and the focus on hegemony.[15] There is also the Lukácsian problematic of revolutionary class consciousness as the key to social change. Further, there are important non-Marxist approaches pertaining to the problem, such as Foucault's theses on the 'order of discourse' in society,[16] the Weberian problematic of 'legitimation', recently spreading into Marxist or Marxisant discourse, particularly in the United States and West Germany; and then there is the question of 'consensus'. After outlining the contours of a materialist theory of ideology, I will try to come to terms with these other approaches as well.

I
The Ideological Formation
of Human Subjects

1. The General Dialectic of Ideology

The operation of ideology in human life basically involves the constitution and patterning of how human beings live their lives as conscious, reflecting initiators of acts in a structured, meaningful world. Ideology operates as discourse, addressing or, as Althusser puts it, interpellating human beings as subjects.

Before setting out to explore how ideology operates in the formation of human subjects and of forms of subjectivity, a note of clarification will be needed concerning the relationship of these processes to those of personality formation. The subjectivity of a person, his/her acting as a particular subject in a particular context, should be distinguished from his/her personality or character structure. Personality and subjectivity each have their specificity, and they have both an autonomy from and effects upon each other.

'Personality' or 'character structure' is being used here as a broad and loose designation of the results of psychodynamic processes studied by psychoanalysis and competing psychological theories. These processes operate upon a material — the libidinal energies and desires of pre-subject infants — and through largely unconscious mechanisms outside the competence of social science and historiography. Personality formation more or less coincides in time with the first subject-formation of human beings, and ideological interpellations constitute an important part of it. But the personality has a temporality of its own, with crucial stages of psychic development and enduring effects depending on how these stages were passed.

A person acts out, lives his/her personality as a subject, in different forms of subjectivity, which nevertheless do not exhaust it. Under certain conditions the two may even come into tension or conflict. The forms of human subjectivity are constituted by intersections of the psychic and the social, and may be seen as the outer, more conscious, and more socially changeable aspects of the person.

Althusser has presented the basic functioning of all ideology as a quadruple system involving: '1. the interpellation of "individuals" as subjects; 2. their subjection to the Subject; 3. the mutual recognition of subjects and Subject, the subjects' recognition of each other, and finally the subject's recognition of himself; 4. the absolute guarantee that everything really is so, and that on condition that the subjects recognize what they are and behave accordingly, everything will be all right: Amen — "So be it"'[17]

He illustrates this system by reference to Jewish and Christian religious ideology, where God (Yahweh) is the Subject with a capital S. This schema appears to me deficient in one crucial respect. It allows no room for any dialectic of ideology. However, such a dialectic is already indicated by the basic ambiguity of the word 'subject', both in French and in English, as Althusser himself suggests without bringing the point clearly into focus. The dialectical character of all ideology may be seen as indicated by the opposite senses of the same word 'subject' in the expressions 'the subject of king X (or the social order Y)' and 'the subjects of history'. In the former sense 'subjects' refers to people who are subjugated under a particular force or order, in the latter to the makers or creators of something.

While retaining the couplet interpellation-recognition, I would suggest that 'subjection-guarantee' be replaced with *subjection-qualification*. The formation of humans by every ideology, conservative or revolutionary, oppressive or emancipatory, according to whatever criteria, involves a process simultaneously of subjection and of qualification. The amorphous libido and manifold potentialities of human infants are subjected to a particular order that allows or favours certain drives and capacities, and prohibits or disfavours others. At the same time, through the same process, new members become qualified to take up and perform (a particular part of) the repertoire of roles given in the society into which they are born, including the role of possible agents of social change. The ambiguity of the words 'qualify' and 'qualification' should also be noted. Although qualified by ideological interpellations, subjects also become qualified to 'qualify' these in return, in the sense of specifying them and modifying their range of application.

The reproduction of any social organization, be it an exploitative society or a revolutionary party, entails a basic correspondence between subjection and qualification. Those who have been subjected to a particular patterning of their capacities, to a particular discipline, qualify for the given roles and are capable of carrying them out. But there is always an inherent possibility that a contradiction may develop between the two. New kinds of qualification may be required and provided, new skills that clash with the traditional forms of subjection. Or, conversely, new forms of subjection may develop that clash with the provision of still-needed qualifications. The effects of a contradiction between subjection and qualification are opposition and revolt or underperformance and withdrawal.

The double process of subjection and qualification involves interpellation by, and recognition in, a central Subject — be it God, Father, Reason, Class, or something more diffuse — that patterns the super-ego of the subjects and provides them with ego-ideals. Given the societal and political orientation of this essay, I will not deal with all the psychoanalytic and linguistic aspects of these processes,[18] but will instead turn to the basic social functioning of subjection-qualification. This involves *three fundamental modes of ideological interpellation*. Ideologies subject and qualify subjects by telling them, relating them to, and making them recognize:

1. *what exists*, and its corollary, what does not exist: that is, who we are, what the world is, what nature, society, men and women are like. In this way we acquire a sense of identity, becoming conscious of what is real and true; the visibility of the world is thereby structured by the distribution of spotlights, shadows, and darkness.

2. *what is good*, right, just, beautiful, attractive, enjoyable, and its opposites. In this way our desires become structured and norm-alized.

3. *what is possible* and impossible; our sense of the mutability of our being-in-the-world and the consequences of change are hereby patterned, and our hopes, ambitions, and fears given shape.

These modes of interpellation have important temporal and spatial dimensions. Thus, interpellations of what exists include both ideologies of what *has existed* and a timing of the present as part of a (backward or forward) trend, a cycle or an infinite immobility. 'What is possible' may range from the endlessness of mere conceivability to the presence of actuality. In the case of ideologies of what is good and right it may be space rather than time that is crucial. Something may be good and just everywhere, somewhere, here, or elsewhere.

The totality of these three modes of interpellation constitute the elementary structure of ideological subjection-qualification, but in any given discourse or discursive strategy they may be allocated different weight and prominence. Viewed from the standpoint of their functioning in social conservation or change, the three modes of interpellation form a logical chain of significance.

Three successive lines of defence of a given order can be established. First, it can be argued that certain features of this order exist while others do not: for example, affluence, equality, and freedom, but not poverty, exploitation, and oppression. (The features selected usually depend on prevailing ideologies of what is just.) Second, if this line of defence no longer holds, and the existence of negative features has to be admitted, it can be argued that what exists is nevertheless just, for example, because the poor and the powerless are misfits and failures who deserve what they get and have only themselves to blame. Third, even the existence of injustice may (have to) be admitted, but then it can be argued that a more just order is not possible, or at least not now. Corresponding to this logic of conservation, there is also a logic of change. In order to become committed to changing something, one must first get to know that it exists, then make up one's mind whether it is good that it exists. And before deciding to do something about a bad state of affairs, one must first be convinced that there is some chance of actually changing it. The time-scale, of course, is crucial to estimates and conceptions of possibility.

These three interpellations and their reception tend to be empirically intertwined, but the unravelling of their internal logic highlights some important flaws and omissions in the traditional approach to ideologies and power. The liberal approach to the study of political ideologies, including the preoccupation with 'consensus' and 'legitimation', has usually concentrated exclusively on the second mode of interpellation, conceptions of the good society, form of government or regime, ignoring the patterning of knowledge and ignorance, and of ambitions, hopes, and fears. The traditional Marxist concern with 'class consciousness' has tended to focus exclusively on the first two aspects of the ideological formation, neglecting the third. But it is, of course, quite possible to be a highly class-conscious member of an exploited class without seeing any concrete possibility of putting an end to one's exploitation. The formation of subjects of class struggle involves, as far as members of exploited classes are concerned, a process of subjection-qualification such that the tasks of producing surplus labour are performed and the existence of class rule is recognized together with its unjust character and the possibility of resisting it. On the part of members of the exploiting class, the formation of class-struggle subjects requires a subjection-qualification to performing the tasks of exploitation, a recognition that this is the right thing to do and that it can be defended.

2. Subjectivity and Role: a Brief Digression on Role Theory

We started this chapter with a note on the relationship between the subject and forms of subjectivity, and personality. We will continue it by briefly spelling out how the concepts used here relate to another concept, that of 'role'. Whereas the question of personality took us to the border of psychology and psychoanalysis, 'role' leads us to sociology and social psychology.

Definitions of 'role' abound in the academic disciplines of sociology and social psychology. Generally, however, it refers to the behaviour normatively expected of persons occupying a particular social position.[19] It is a key concept in Parsonian and much post-Parsonian sociology. The social-psychological focus on personal behaviour and inter-personal relations in terms of role-definitions and role-enactment usually goes under the name of role theory. On at least some occasions when forms of subjectivity have here been talked about a mainstream sociologist or a social-psychologist would probably have talked about roles. What is the rationale for the introduction of a new concept in this essay?

Three reasons are of prime importance. First, the sociological concept of role is embedded in a particular conception of society, an idealist and personalist view, in which social behaviour is seen as exclusively normatively defined and social relations as interpersonal relations only. What is lost here is class and the materiality of economic relations and technology. Role-theorists talk of occupational but not of class roles, and rightly so, since there is no normative definition of classes in capitalist society, no normative definition of surplus labour and surplus-labour extraction. Only outside the sociological problematic of ideological community may we talk of class 'roles', defined by specific relations of production and functioning on the basis of particular forces of production. Second, the 'role'-problematic is one of given individuals responding to given social demands. Its orientation, therefore, is basically static. Inherent in the double sense of 'subject', on the other hand, is the always present possibility of transcendence of social and personal givens. For example, we can talk of subjects of class struggle and subjects of social change, but hardly of 'roles' in the same context. Third, the 'role'-problematic is profoundly non-dialectical. It focuses on role-definitions, role-learning, role-performance and external conflicts — between personality and role-expectations or between different possible roles of the same individual. The problematic of subject and forms of subjectivity, by contrast, highlights the intrinsic unity *and* possible conflict of the opposite processes of subjection and qualification.

3. The Ideological Universe: the Dimensions of Human Subjectivity

If we are to progress towards a firm and systematic understanding of the relationship between class and ideology, and, more broadly, of what determines the generation and articulation of ideologies, then we must try to draw a structural map of the universe of ideologies as a whole. In view of the enormous variety of ideologies, past and present this may seem an utterly impossible attempt, doomed to inglorious failure. Nevertheless, the risk will be taken. Of course, any attempt to structure the ideological universe can be made only at a very high level of abstraction. But insofar as it can be shown to be exhaustive, it may enable us to locate the problem of class ideology in a systematic and comprehensive framework.

We have defined the operation of ideology in terms of the constitution of human subjectivity, and it follows then that to search for the structure of the ideological universe is to seek the dimensions of human subjectivity. At the most general level, it appears that two such dimensions of man's being-in-the-world as a conscious subject can be distinguished. These may in turn be ordered along two axes, one referring to 'being', the other to 'in-the-world'. Thus, 'being' a human subject is something *existential* — being a sexed individual at a particular point of one's life cycle related to other sexed individuals of different generations at a certain point of their life cycle ('existential' seems more adequate than 'biological' to designate the first aspect of being, since we are concerned with its subjectively meaningful side). It is also something *historical* — being a person who exists only in certain human societies at a particular point in human history, say a shaman, tax farmer, blacksmith, or footballer. Being 'in the world' is both *inclusive* (being a member of a meaningful world) and *positional* (having a particular place in the world in relation to other members of it, having a particular gender and age, occupation, ethnicity, and so on).

My thesis is that these four dimensions make up the fundamental forms of human subjectivity, and that the universe of ideologies is exhaustively structured by the four main types of interpellation that constitute these four forms of subjectivity. We may illustrate the structure of the ideological universe by means of the following simple four-fold table.

The Universe of Ideological Interpellations

Subjectivities of 'in-the-world'	Subjectivities of 'being'	
	Existential	*Historical*
Inclusive	1	2
Positional	3	4

Since no words of sufficient generality seem available, the four main types of ideology are provisionally designated only by numbers. The next task, then, is to remove the cover of anonymity from these numbers: to concretize their synonyms, the inclusive-existential, the inclusive-historical, the positional-existential and the positional-historical.

1. *Inclusive-Existential Ideologies.* This type of ideological discourse provides meanings related to being a member of the world, i.e., the meaning of life, suffering, death, the cosmos, and the natural order. It concerns what life is, what

is good and bad in life, what is possible in human existence, and whether there is a life after bodily death. The most common forms of discourse treating these questions are mythologies, religions, and secular moral discourse. They can vary greatly, not only in content but also in elaboration, from the grand mythological and religious systems to the very diffuse and often tacit conceptions of a life-purpose provided in the secularized societies of contemporary advanced capitalism.

2. *Inclusive-Historical Ideologies.* Through these, human beings are constituted as conscious members of historical social worlds. These social worlds are indefinite in number and variety, and it is only for purposes of illustration that we might mention the forms of tribe, village, ethnicity, state, nation, church. Bourgeois political theory usually concentrates on such entities, addressing the members (citizens) of the state, in contrast to the positional address to the prince typical of feudal ideologists. Bourgeois political theory tells the citizens what the state is, what is good and bad politics and what is politically possible or impossible. Virtually anything can define membership in a social world. Furthermore, definitions and demarcations of social worlds overlap, compete, and clash with one another. Medieval European political history, for instance, was to a large extent a history of the competition between the overlapping social worlds of dynastic states and the Church. It should also be noted that membership of one social world not only conflicts with membership in others, but also coexists with them in varying hierarchies of domination and subordination. For instance, one may be, simultaneously, a conscious US citizen, a Catholic, an Italian, a member of the working class, a resident of a particular neighbourhood, and a member of a particular kin group.

Since inclusive ideologies define membership in a meaningful world and thereby draw a line of demarcation between membership and non-membership, they are also ideologies of *exclusion*. 'Excluded' here may refer, for example, to a life devoid of meaning (however defined), estrangement from God, not-belonging to the tribe, ethnicity, nation, state, and so on.

3. *Positional-Existential Ideologies.* A positional ideology subjects one to, and qualifies one for, a particular position in the world of which one is a member. The most significant positions of the existential world, the most important aspects of the structure of givens in human existence, are those delineated by the Self-Others and the two-genders distinctions and by the life-cycle of childhood, youth, maturity, and old age. Positional-existential ideologies, then, constitute subject-forms of individuality, (fe)maleness, of age and ageing. Hereby they tell one who one is in contrast with others, what is good and what is possible for one.

4. *Positional-Historical Ideologies.* Human beings also occupy positions in historical social worlds. Historical-positional ideologies form the members of a family in a structure of families and lineages, the inhabitants of a particular locality in a wider pattern of social geography, the occupants of a particular educational status, the practitioners of particular occupations and of particular life-styles, the incumbents of positions of political power (and the place of those without it), the members of different classes. Positions may be differentiated and linked in terms of difference only, in terms of hierarchical grading along a single continuum of criteria, of complementarity, competition, and frontal conflict.

Three important aspects of the ideological universe should be noted. First, the distinctions made above are analytical. They do not represent ideologies as they concretely appear and are labelled in everyday language.

These may exhibit more than one of the four dimensions, either at the same time or in different contexts. A religious ideology, for instance, is not only an inclusive-existential ideology. In a multi-religious or a partly secularized society it also operates as a historical-positional ideology. Nationalism may be both an inclusive- and a positional-historical ideology, in the latter form constituting subjects of a position within an international system; the main accent of a given nationalist ideology may lie on one or the other. Inversely, in some tendencies of the labour movement, particularly revolutionary anarcho-syndicalism, 'class' becomes more an inclusive than a positional ideology. The adversary is seen not so much as occupying a position of domination within a particular mode of production, as an alien, superfluous body outside the class of producers. In this perspective the revolution is seen more as a displacement or deportation of alien parasites than as a transformation of society. As one prominent Spanish Anarchist put it, 'after the revolution . . . the workers will have to do the same as they did the day before'.[20] Second, I would claim that the types of ideology identified are exhaustive and irreducible. One implication of this, particularly important for Marxists to keep in mind, is that the ideological universe is never reducible to class ideologies. Even in the most class-polarized and class-conscious societies, the other fundamental forms of human subjectivity coexist with class subjectivities. Inescapably, the sex- and age-specificities of human individuals are ideologically constituted by existential-positional ideologies. And the meaning of a person's life and world is an existential question not wholly answerable by reference to the relations of production, but rather addressed by the inclusive-existential ideologies of religion and secular morality.

It will also have to be kept in mind that positional ideologies by definition always refer to positions within a broader world, held in common with incumbents of other positions. A class, for instance, forms part both of a common mode of production together with its opposite exploiting or exploited class and/or (the latter in the case of the petty bourgeoisie and patriarchal peasants, each supporting a non-exploitative mode of production) exists within a historical social formation composed of several classes. It is, then, natural — and not an aberration of underdeveloped class consciousness — that class ideologies coexist with inclusive-historical ideologies, constituting the subjects of the contradictory totality of an exploitative mode of production and/or social formation.

Third, the irreducible multidimensionality of ideologies means that a crucial aspect of ideological struggles and of ideological relations of force is the articulation of a given type of ideology with others. The efficacy of a given religion, for example, will have to be understood in its articulation, explicit or implicit, with historical ideologies, positional and inclusive. In the labour movement the strategic conception of the ideological class struggle over the articulation of class with other kinds of ideology was elaborated by Kollontai and Reich with reference to existential ideologies, and it was Gramsci above all who explored the articulations of inclusive national ideologies.

4. Ego- and Alter-Ideologies

There is a further aspect of ideologies and their operation that writers on ideology have rarely paid attention to. Positional ideologies have an intrinsically dual character: in one's subjection-to-and-qualification-for a particular position, one becomes aware of the difference between oneself and the others. Now, this distinction is particularly relevant insofar as the ideology of dominating subjects is concerned, since 'domination' designates precisely a particular and crucial relationship to the Other. Male-chauvinist sexist ideology should thus be seen as both an ego-ideology of maleness and an alter-ideology of femaleness. (This duality is inherent in every gender-specific subjectivity and is not necessarily sexist.) The same is true of positional-historical ideology. The ideology of a ruling bourgeoisie, for example, should be analysed both as an ego-ideology, forming the subjects of the bourgeoisie itself, and as an alter-ideology, dominating or striving to dominate the formation of other class subjects. In isolated primitive communities the inclusive ideologies tended to have no alter-dimension, what was outside their own world being chaos or nothingness. In more developed and interrelated social worlds, however, inclusive ideologies also have an alter-component in the 'infidels', the 'heathens', the 'aliens', and so on.

Alter-ideologies refer to the ideological dimension of the form in which one relates to the Other: to perceptions of the Other and of one's relationship to him/her. In relationships of power and domination, the alter-ideology of the dominating subjects is translated into attempts to mould the dominated according to the rulers' image of them, and into resistance to the opposition of the ruled. It is in this way that domination is ensured. The alter-ideology of the dominated, on the other hand, while also involving a perception and evaluation of the differences between ego and alter, tends towards resistance to the Other rather than towards forming him or her. This difference is inscribed in the asymmetry of domination.

Students of race or ethnic relations and of sexism have long recognized this duality in ideologies, though often without explicitly theorizing it. Much less attention has been paid to it in class analysis, but it is essential to an understanding of the ideological constitution of the subjects of class struggle and class collaboration.

II
The Historical Materialism
of Ideologies

The question of the *material determination of ideology* is central to historical materialism (and to some other theories as well, like utilitarianism and the 'sociology of knowledge'). In the classical tradition this question was approached with the help of the 'base-superstructure' metaphor. But in contemporary Western Marxism not only the metaphor but also the question itself has tended to be cast aside. In the Althusserian tradition, emphasis was laid, first, on the science/ideology demarcation, then on ideology 'in general' and the operation of 'ideological state apparatuses'. In the neo-Gramscian problematic the emphasis has been on the creation and organization of ideological hegemony, seen primarily as a question of strategic political choice rather than as something whose possibilities are socially determined. Others still have had recourse to the Weberian conception of legitimacy, directing their interest to 'crises of legitimation' in the social order. Now, for Marxists this question of material determination cannot simply be bypassed. It is central to the corpus of historical-materialist theory, and has to be confronted, directly and explicitly.[21]

The explanatory tasks of a materialist theory of ideologies are twofold, concerning the *generation and change of ideologies* and the *patterning of the relationships between given ideologies*, relationships of predominance, interdependence and subordination. The first, not broached at all in Althusser's essay, refers to the formation of new and the changes of existing forms of human subjectivity. The second aspect Althusser has analysed by means of the concept of 'ideological state apparatuses'. However, apart from the problem with the concept itself, this part of his theory is unrelated to his two other poles of analysis. It is not on a par with his theory of 'ideology in general', because ideology is a constituent part of all human societies whereas the state is not. On the other hand, it is not theoretically located in the analysis of historical social formations — though his illustrations refer to them — since the overall argument is structured around the reproductive logic of an exploitative mode of production.

1. The Structure of Ideological Systems

Let us start with a given system of ideologies and look at its patterning. We will first state two general propositions concerning its determination: one historical, the second material.

Proposition One: All ideologies exist only in historical forms in historical degrees of salience and modes of articulation with other ideologies.

This means that, while they are not reducible to the temporality of human history, existential ideologies operate only in historically determined forms. Today this may not be a very daring or original proposition, but at the time of the founders of historical materialism it was still very controversial. It went against the natural-law conceptions of bourgeois individualism, with its 'natural' or 'self-evident' individual rights, as well as against absolutist conceptions of religion as eternal, divine truth. Individuality, (fe)maleness, religious doctrine and secular morality exist only in particular historical patterns and in articulation with historical-positional and historical-inclusive ideologies. These patterns are, then, subject to historical change, though the existence of existential ideology *per se* is not. One implication of this proposition would be that the operation of, say, Roman Catholicism across centuries and continents — its practice, acceptance or rejection and the struggles over it — has to be analysed in terms of its articulation with different historical ideologies and historical social forces.

Proposition Two: All ideologies operate in a material matrix of affirmations and sanctions, and this matrix determines their interrelationships.

All human activity is invested with meaning and all ideological interpellations have some kind of 'material' existence, in bodily movements, sounds, paper and ink, and so on. This does not mean, however, that it is impossible to distinguish, analytically, ideological from material, discursive from non-discursive dimensions of human practices. After all, there is some difference between being pronounced 'dead' by a hostile critic and being assassinated. We can, then, distinguish between practices in which the discursive dimension is dominant, like making a speech or writing an essay on ideology, and others in which the non-discursive predominates, like making love, war, revolution or automobiles. Provided we keep in mind that we are *distinguishing* analytically predominant dimensions and not substantially *separating* empirically intertwined phenomena, we may draw a shorthand distinction between discursive and non-discursive practices.

Against this background, I would argue that one aspect of the material determination of ideologies is brought about by the matrix of non-discursive practices in which the operation of every ideology is inscribed. A historical-materialist conception of ideology, it would seem, involves the not very far-fetched assumption that human beings tend to have some capacity for discriminating between enunciation of the existence or possibility of something, or of its goodness according to given criteria, and the actual existence/occurrence of what is enunciated. In other words, ordinary human beings are capable of judging, at least under certain circumstances, whether a statement that the sun is shining, or that there is no unemployment, is true.

The material matrix of any ideology can be analysed as operating through *affirmations* and *sanctions*, such that ideologies become effective by being related to the one or the other. In an affirming practice, if an interpellated subject acts in accordance with the dictates of ideological discourse, then the outcome predicted by ideology occurs; while if the subject contravenes the dictates of ideological discourse, then he or she is sanctioned, through failure, unemployment, bankruptcy, imprisonment, death, or whatever. Parental love and punishment form another important part of the affirmation/sanctioning of ideologies — though not unfailingly, as is well known.

At this point we should recall the content of my argument about the matrix of affirmations and sanctions: the determination of the relationship between given ideologies as one of domination and subordination, relative growth, reinforcement, marginalization, and decline. The material matrix operates not as a *ménage à trois* involving men, ideology, and reality, but as a determinant in the competition and clash between different ideologies, between different interpretations of reality or different interpellations concerning what exists, is good, and is possible. If every ideology operates within a matrix of affirmations and sanctions, then the competition, coexistence or conflict of different ideologies is dependent on the non-discursive matrices. The power of a given ideology in relation to others is determined by its pertinent affirmations and sanctions. However, all ideologies tend to have defence mechanisms that try to explain, or 'explain away', the non-occurrence of affirmations or sanctions. Specialized mechanisms of this sort, which tend to develop in all institutionalized ideologies, include symbolic affirmations and sanctions, rites or ritual practices; that is, particular non-discursive practices that have a meaning only within a given ideological discourse. Furthermore, institutionalized ideologies tend also to possess an important internal sanction: *excommunication*, often with the support of non-discursive sanctions.

There is one historically important form of ideology that poses special problems about its affirming-sanctioning matrix — supranaturalist religion. Karl Kautsky, whose classic *The Foundations of Christianity* is still one of the few Marxist works on religion, tells an illustrative story from the age of Marcus Aurelius. A Roman army, encircled by a superior enemy, was suffering from heat and thirst under a blistering sun. Suddenly rain started to fall upon the Romans and an awe-inspiring thunderstorm broke over the enemy. The imperial army was saved. How was the event seen in this age of competitive religion? To some, it was the action of Jupiter to whom the Emperor had appealed. Others gave thanks to Hermes, whom an Egyptian magician had conjured into action, while Christians saw the miracle as a vindication of their God, to whom the soldiers of the Twelfth Legion had prayed. Although the evidence of this particular case appears too thin to settle the dispute, it may be argued that the worldly fate of religious discourses is decided by their relationship to the non-discursive dimensions of mundane reality. In this respect there are at least two different questions. One is the religious phenomenon *per se* as an ideological form, the other is the importance of a particular religion in a particular society at a particular point in time. Religions seem to derive their essential impetus from: (a) the answers they give to existential questions about the conscious human condition and the meaning of life; (b) their 'explanation' of historical origins, the natural order and contemporary events; and (c) the power they impart by affording 'true' knowledge of what governs the world. The first thrives above all on changes in material conditions that affirm the urgency of such existential questions as human suffering. The second and the third depend most directly on the lack or uncertainty of more mundane historical and natural explanations and technologies of production and control.

The victory of a certain religion over other ideologies always involves social struggles — whatever extra-terrestrial forces may be struggling as well. Therefore, the most immediate determinant in affirming a certain religion and sanctioning its rivals is the superior mundane power of the social forces with which it has become linked. The power of Christianity in the Roman Empire was decided by the victory of Constantine's army over Maxenius, and Islam was later spread by the victorious Arab sword. This intimate link between celestial and earthly power was tellingly expressed in the principle of settlement at the time of the Continental European wars of religion: *eius religio, cuius regio* (he who governs determines the religion).

However, even a brief aside on the material matrix of religions cannot rest content with this observation. We also know that religions have arisen and spread among the downtrodden and oppressed, and have gathered strength by their linkage with forces of social and/or national opposition. There is not only the religion of the existing powers, but also religious-cum-social dissent, as evidenced by the early Christians, the medieval German Anabaptists, the English Puritans, the reinforcement of Irish Catholicism under British rule, the Islamic revival in Iran during the

Shah's last period in power. To be able to account for these phenomena as well, we have to sketch the contours of the material affirmations and sanctions of religions somewhat more systematically.

On a very general level, religions constitute an alternative to naturalist sense-making of the world and to secularized morality. The latter derive their strength from the affirmations and sanctions discovered by natural science and produced by human organization, capitalist industry and markets, working-class collective organization. Before their development the life of the masses was largely governed by inscrutable natural constraints and calamities. These mysterious governing forces could then more easily be given sense by the invocation of divine powers. Up to the bourgeois revolutions of the late-eighteenth and nineteenth centuries, religion constituted the dominant idiom for defining the meaning of the world.

Religions may further be materially affirmed by what they say or imply about the earthly capacities and practices of their respective non-believers, about their lack of power but also about their oppressive exercise of it, about their corruption or their misery. Religions may be affirmed by the mundane everyday succour of the preachers and the parish, and by the earthly effects of obeying the religious moral code. They may derive strength from the redress of material grievances, or from the defence of worldly positions that they promise, explicitly or implicitly. Religions have their deepest roots in the existential aspects of human subjectivity. But the strength or weakness of supranaturalist religion as well as the spread and decline of particular denominations and creeds are governed by their earthly affirmations and sanctions in their confrontations with other existential ideologies, religious or secular.

These two general propositions concerning the historicity and materiality of ideology, do not, of course, amount to a historical-materialist theory of ideology in the strict Marxian sense. Historical materialism also asserts a class determination of ideologies: 'the ruling ideas of an epoch are always those of the ruling class'. If we accept the basic tenets of historical materialism, while rejecting the utilitarian traces in Marx and Engels, this thesis must entail at least two further propositions about the structuring of a given set of ideologies.

Proposition Three: All ideologies (in class societies) exist in historical forms of articulation with different classes and class ideologies.

This means that forms of individuality, (fe)maleness, religion, secular morality, geographic and ethnic positionality, and nationalism, are bound up with and affected by different modes of class existence and are linked to and affected by different class ideologies. According to this proposition male chauvinism, for instance, should be understood — and, from a non-sexist perspective, combated — in its links with different class modes of existence, class practices and class ideological discourses. But it does not entail that male chauvinism is the ideology and practice of the members of one class only.

Proposition Four: The patterning of a given set of ideologies is (within class societies) overdetermined by class relations of strength and by the class struggle.

This is the crucial and the most controversial proposition of historical materialism in this context. To sceptical minds it would require a long, empirically corroborated argument, impossible within the limits of this essay. Here I will have to confine myself to spelling out its meaning and implications.

The affirming and sanctioning matrix of ideologies is part of the system of economic and political power in a given society. Historical materialism analyses the system of economic power in terms of the mode(s) of production on the bases of which classes, the agents of specific economic practices, are defined. Political power is seen as a condensation of the totality of social power relations — fundamentally, of class relations — and as crystallized in a particular institution, the state.

Ideological conflicts and competition are (usually) not directly determined by class relations and the class struggle. They operate through specific forms of social organization and process. Moreover, non-class ideologies have a historicity and a materiality that are intrinsically not reducible to those of the mode(s) of production. But as we have asserted, in Proposition Three, non-class ideologies are always linked with classes, and all ideologies are inscribed in an overall system of social power constituted by conflicting classes of varying strength. In this sense, the structure of the ideological system, its class and non-class elements alike, is overdetermined by the constellation of class forces.

'Class overdetermination' of an ideological structure means, to use an apt conceptualization developed by Erik Olin Wright, that different classes *select* different forms of non-class ideologies and that class constellations of force *limit* the possibilities of ideological interrelationships and of ideological change. Proposition Four implies, for instance, that if we want to explain the different relative positions of Catholicism and nationalism in contemporary France and Italy, we should look at how these ideologies have been linked with different classes, and at the outcome of the struggles between these classes. Nationalism became linked with the bourgeois revolution, as a revolutionary rallying-cry and weapon against the dynastic state and its principle of dynastic legitimacy. The Catholic Church and the Papacy, on the other hand, were historically closely allied with the dynastic state and its dominant social forces. Catholicism therefore became a banner of the counter-revolutionaries and their clienteles. The radical and victorious revolution of the French bourgeoisie and petty-bourgeoisie may then be seen to have led to the triumph of nationalism, whereas the weaker and more moderate bourgeois revolution in Italy would explain a much stronger Catholic legacy. The bourgeois and the petty-bourgeois classes on one hand, and the quasi-feudal classes on the other might be seen as having 'selected' nationalism and Catholicism, respectively, in a particular conjuncture (which then cancelled the reverse options), and their respective strengths and weaknesses as having posed 'limits' to supra-nationalist and secular ideologies.

The four propositions stated above do not share a single theoretical status. My own view is that the first two, concerning the historicity and the determining material matrix of all ideologies, are basic to any scientific study of the functioning of ideologies. The third, that in class societies all ideologies are differently linked with different classes, is an immensely fruitful guide to research and understanding which should always be kept in mind; while the last proposition — the structure of an ideological system is overdetermined by the class struggle — should perhaps be treated as a very important and fruitful hypothesis, whose explanatory power will remain an open question in any given empirical study.

2. The Generation of Ideologies and Material Change

A materialist theory of ideology will also have to confront the question: Where do ideologies come from? or, How did this particular ideology originate? A simple (or rather, naive) materialist answer would be: from the economic base. However, if we go through Marx's own formulations on the material determination of ideologies, in *The Communist Manifesto*, *The Eighteenth Brumaire*, the Preface to *A*

Contribution to the Critique of Political Economy, Capital and *Theories of Surplus Value*, we will find that the architectural metaphor *per se* was not his central focus. Rather, his crucial point was that the ideological universe is predominantly class-determined, by class practices, class experiences, class ideologies and class power. Classes in turn are defined as the occupants of definite positions in the economic mode of production, the structure and dynamics of which determine the practices, experiences, ideologies, and power of different classes. About how this class determination operated Marx had relatively little to say. His clearest formulations were probably those of the third volume of *Capital* referring to the everyday economic conceptions of the capitalists, arising out of their practices and experiences as competitive market agents.

A century later we should not be contented with interpreting Marx. We should use him, for theoretical and political development and change. I will therefore take Marx's insights as a point of departure for an attempt at a more systematic theory. The explanatory pattern of determination within historical materialism is constituted by the combination of the forces and the relations of production and the classes determined by it. The following eight propositions will try to delimit what historical materialism can and cannot claim to explain about the generation of ideologies.

Proposition One: The generation of ideologies in human societies is always, from the point of view of social science and historiography, a process of change of pre-existing ideologies.

Proposition Two: Ideological change, and the generation of ideologies, is always dependent upon non-ideological, material change.

Proposition Three: The most important material change is

constituted by the internal social dynamics of societies and of their modes of production.

Proposition Four: Every mode of production requires specific economic positional ideologies, and every exploitative mode of production specific class ideologies.

Proposition Five: Every new mode of production will generate new economic positional ideologies.

Proposition Six: All human societies exhibit existential- and historical-inclusive as well as historical-positional ideologies.

Proposition Seven: The concrete forms of existential, historical-inclusive and historical-positional ideologies other than the economic are not directly determined by the mode of production, but changes in the former are over-determined by the latter.

Proposition Eight: New modes of production and new classes will generate forms of existential, historical-inclusive and other historical-positional ideologies that are capable of supporting and reinforcing the new predominant class ideologies, if the former do not already exist.

As the reader will have noticed, the traditional base-superstructure problematic has been considerably reformulated here. As a simple relationship it figures only in Proposition Four, and then only in a functional argument: a mode of production requires a certain kind of ideology, alongside others, for human subjects to be able to perform its tasks. Instead the focus is on the determination of ideological change, for it seems that only in this way can the question of 'base and superstructure' escape circularity. Further, the fundamental problems of material determination have to be recast in the light of two fundamental considerations.

Any social-scientific and social-historical theory and analysis has to start from the 'always-already-constituted' existence of human society. Neither social science nor historiography can account for all the processes of evolution from groups of ape-like primates to societies of humans. A corollary is that any theoretical inquiry into the generation of ideologies will have to start by looking at the prerequisites for the reproduction and change of already existing ideologies in a given society, and for the generation of new ideologies from an existing set of ideologies and social relations. Furthermore, the ideological formation of a given set of human beings does not start from their confrontation with a particular natural and social environment, but from their being the offspring of particular mothers and familial relations in a particular society.

From what is known about the ideological plasticity of human beings and their creative capacities, we should expect the given ideologies to be almost completely reproduced in societies whose internal conditions and relationships to the natural environment and to other societies remain exactly the same from one generation to the next. (We would have to allow for only a small margin of individual 'misfits' stemming from the irreducibility of psychodynamic processes to complete social control.) A parental generation will always mould its children according to its own form of subjectivity; and if the ecological, demographic, socio-economic and any inter-societal relationships remain the same, the younger generation will face exactly the same affirmations and sanctions of the existing ideologies as the parental one. It follows that the explanation/investigation of the generation of ideologies will have to start from *processes of change in the structure of a given society and in its relationships to its natural environment and to other societies.* It is *these changes* that *constitute the material determination of the rise of ideologies.*

Idealist conceptions of history seem to be based implicitly on two dubious assumptions. First, they rely on what we might call the 'Munchhausen effect': the capacity of human beings to pull themselves up by their ideological bootstraps. This assumes that, simply through the power of ideological imagination, each new generation of humans can emancipate itself from ideological formation by its parents, even though facing exactly the same situations as the latter. Second, they presuppose that existential ideologies, among which primordial significance is usually given to the inclusive ideologies of religion and moral philosophy, themselves stand outside history but can — and do — none the less act as the movers of history. This is untenable.

The variety of forms of individuality, of male- and femaleness, of religion and morality, shows that existential ideologies always exist in concrete historical forms, but are never reducible to them. These historically determined existential ideologies must then be subject to the same laws of reproduction and change as all other ideologies. Further, idealist theories of history have usually focused on and attached overriding significance to ideological interpellations of what is good and right (and their opposites). But it follows from the intergenerational perspective on ideological formation that interpellations and experiences of what is, and of what is possible, are more important than changes of ideologies of what is good and right. They overdetermine such changes, even if they never fully absorb them.

The historical materialist conception of ideology, however, involves two further, quite fundamental, specifications of the general materialist conception. First, it implies that internal social dynamics, rather than natural phenomena like climatic change or natural disasters, are the most important key to change in a given society; that the internal social dynamic is governed by forces and relations of production rather than by, say, demographic food/

population ratios; and that the character and outcome of co-operation and conflict between societies — for example, the likelihood and the effects of conquest and subjugation — are mainly determined by the internal structure of the societies in question. Expressed in terms of our structural schema of the ideological universe, this means that the history of ideologies is not one of the victories and defeats, domination and subordination, of inclusive historical social ideologies: it is not the history of a succession of victorious and dominant *Volksgeister*.

When a given set of ideologies is reproduced in unchanged form, its overall matrix is a constant totality of social, eco-social, and inter-societal relations in which the enunciations of the parent generation are affirmed for the children's generation and any violations are sanctioned, in the same way as they were for the parent generation itself. Any changes in this totality, which form the matrix of the generation of ideological change, may be grouped into two basic categories. The first may be termed *disarticulating uneven developments*, that is, any developments that tend to fracture the previous totality — from demographic trends affecting the relation between population and means of subsistence to the appearance of new and powerful neighbours. The second of these categories is *contradictions*. Although in Marxist discourse this word is often extended to cover any kind of conflict, it should properly be restricted to the development of a particular kind of conflict, namely, between two elements forming an intrinsic whole. The effect of the development of a social contradiction, then, is to create a 'dilemma'.

Marxism has traditionally focused on one fundamental contradiction: that between the forces and the relations of production, directly pointing towards a change in the position of the classes and in the parameters of their struggle. But it is also quite possible for political and ideological contradictions to develop — contradictions which, as I argued in *What Does the Ruling Class Do When It Rules?*, are essentially located between the relations of social *domination* and the forces of *execution* of societal tasks in the state, and ideologically, between *subjection* and *qualification*. Thus the ideological contradiction does not refer to any lack of logical consistency in a given discourse, which is nearly always of secondary significance to its social efficacy.

Earlier, we identified the process of ideological formation as an intrinsic unity of subjection and qualification. They are two sides of the same process and therefore always tend to correspond; indeed, there are always strategies of power to ensure their correspondence. But a contradiction may arise between the two as the dynamics of a society unfold. Either the subjection of the younger generation — or, if we take a synchronic view, of the dominated population — may for some reason change in form or strength while the tasks for which the new members have to be qualified do not change, or change in a different direction. Or else, there may be a change in the qualifications needed or given, while the forms of subjection do not change accordingly.

Generally, it is the latter form of contradiction that is dangerous to a given order. The former most often tends to produce underperformance, dropping out, or riots, whereas the second has potentially revolutionary implications of social transformation. In many societies with dynastic or colonial forms of subjection, the training of an intelligentsia with the qualifications of an advanced capitalist society has tended to generate revolutionary ideologies and practices. The student movement in the advanced capitalist countries during the late sixties came out of a similar contradiction, involving a massive increase in tertiary education and training to which the old forms of academic subjection no longer effectively corresponded in the given conjuncture. (As we all know, however, given the lack of assertiveness in revolutionary working-class practice, the revolutionary student movement actually fizzled out.) The processes of capitalist de-skilling of workers, vividly pictured by Harry Braverman, can be seen as an attempt to maintain the correspondence of subjection and qualification. However, the basic Marxian hypothesis of social change is that the training of workers as free persons in an increasingly centralized labour-market and in an increasingly collective work process, will tend to conflict with bourgeois subjection and will generate revolutionary socialist ideology and practice.

The three fundamental types of contradiction are not independent, but are all interrelated. Marxism asserts that the political contradiction of domination-execution and the ideological contradictions of subjection-qualification are largely governed by, though not reducible to, the economic correspondence or contradiction between the relations and forces of production. Any given combination of forces and relations of production of course requires a particular form of ideological subjection-qualification of the economic subjects, and tends to ensure it through such sanctions as starvation, unemployment, bankruptcy — and their opposites, which affirm the correctness of the corresponding subjection-qualification. But if a contradiction develops between the relations and forces of production, no ideological formation can adequately and harmoniously subject-qualify the new economic subjects for the contradictory economic order. The old matrix of economic affirmations and sanctions then tends to crack.

Ideologies change and new ideologies emerge and spread when the old matrix of affirmations and sanctions changes through contradictions and other, disarticulating developments. The process of ideological formation does not take place in ideology alone. It is always a subjection to, and a qualification for, a particular social order with non-discursive dimensions. When this order changes, the previous subjection-qualification is no longer adequately affirmed and sanctioned — a fact which tends to lead to more or less radical reformulations whose viability is determined by the extent to which they are then more effectively affirmed and sanctioned.

So far we have only treated three of the eight propositions set out above; these are the basic ones. Proposition Four, concerning the functional necessity of class ideologies, will be treated extensively in the next chapter. Proposition Five, that new modes of production will generate new economic positional ideologies follows from Proposition Four; and that it is thus, and not rather the other way around, follows from Proposition Three. Proposition Six merely repeats what was said in the previous chapter about the ideological universe.

Proposition Seven, that the concrete forms of ideologies other than economic positional ones are not directly determined by the mode of production, indicates the limitations of historical materialism. For example, no theory of the feudal mode of production can explain why feudalism was accompanied in Europe by Catholic Christianity and by Shintoism in Japan. But the assertion that all ideological changes are overdetermined by material ones, implies, at the same time, that the religious schisms and wars in Europe were overdetermined by changes in the class structure and by class politics.

The last proposition, that new modes of production will generate new forms of supporting existential- and historical-inclusive ideologies if they do not already exist, follows in part from what was said in the previous chapter about the historical forms of articulation of different ideologies. Since these ideological changes operate upon very different historical ideological systems, and since the rise of a given mode of production may come about through different

processes of transformation, we should expect the new ideological forms to differ considerably across countries dominated by the same mode of production. Nationalism, for instance, was vigorously and successfully generated both in France and in Germany as part of a struggle against dynastic principles of government, aristocratic institutions and traditional jurisdictions with their barriers to market and state unification. But whereas in France this nationalism developed in the clear-cut bourgeois direction, of Jacobinism and Republicanism with a Bonapartist interlude, in the Wilhelmine Reich bourgeois nationalism became fused with and increasingly subservient to the dynasty and the Junkers.[22]

III
The Ideological Constitution
of Classes

The term 'classes' designates categories of human beings who 'act out', or serve as the 'bearers' of, given relations of production and form the subjects of class struggles. As such, they have to be subjected to and qualified for their class roles, and this subjection-qualification is specific to each particular class. It is thus impossible, from one minute to the next and without any new subjection-qualification, to turn a feudal lord into an industrial worker or a merchant banker into a servile peasant. In this sense Poulantzas was right to emphasize that classes always have a specific ideological, as well as economic, existence. We cannot talk of class struggle, of the struggle of classes ('struggle' of course refers to practices of subjects) as an analytic concept for structuring the myriad of social conflicts, without assuming an ideological constitution of classes by specific class ideologies.[23]

The ideological constitution of classes is a topic for social historiography, from which any theoretical treatment of ideology must learn and to which any full-scale analysis must relate. Let us just mention a few works of this kind: Brunner, Duby, and Joanna on the feudal classes; Thompson, Hobsbawm, Foster, Perrot, Trempe, and Vester on the working class; Genovese on southern US slaves and slave-owners.[24] Less attention has been devoted to the formation of the bourgeoisie, but we should keep in mind at least the well-known works of Tawney and Weber, Bramsted's analysis of the conflicts between and changes in aristocratic and bourgeois ideology in nineteenth-century German literature, Hirschmann's study of early pro-capitalist argumentation, and Baglioni's monograph on the ideology of the Italian industrial bourgeoisie up to the First World War.[25] There is, on the whole, a wealth of historiographical works pertaining to the problem. Empirical sociology has made a significant contribution on the ideological make-up of (sections of) contemporary classes.[26] Important documentation is also readily available in literary works, from Balzac's material on the contrasts between the feudal aristocracy and the bourgeoisie, to Thomas Mann's portrait of the mercantile bourgeoisie in *Buddenbrooks*, to the great generation of autobiographical Swedish proletarian writers of the 1930s. Theoretically presumptious though it may seem to many historians, the essay-framework of the present study obliges me to omit precise historical references.

In any case, it should be stressed that some specifically theoretical tasks have to be solved before the historical evidence can speak to us about the ideological formation of classes. This is so because *the concept of class ideology is not synonymous with the ideological configuration prevailing among the members of a given class at a given time*. It follows from what has been said above that the actual ideological ensemble of the members of a given class is a complex totality of different elements that cannot be reduced to one another. It contains, apart from class ideology, more or less idiosyncratic existential-positional ideologies, existential-inclusive and historical-inclusive ideologies, non-class historical-positional ideologies, and elements of the alter-ideology of other classes. Hence, it must be theoretically determined which ideologies are feudal, bourgeois, proletarian, petty-bourgeois or whatever; this question is not answerable by historical or sociological induction alone.

This necessary theoretical determination must proceed from the class-specific positions defined by the relations of production — from the specific kind of ideological subjection-qualification that they imply. The concept of relations of production denotes, as I have shown elsewhere,[27] three aspects of the social organization of production: i) the mode of distributing the means of production, the channels of access to them and the barriers of separation; ii) the social relationships within and between the producers and the appropriators of surplus labour in the economic mode of production (including its overdetermined aspects of circulation, exchange, revenue distribution, and consumption); iii) the objective or institutionalized orientation of production.

Theoretical determination of specific class ideologies therefore involves finding the minimum subjection-qualification (in terms of interpellations of what exists, what is good, and what is possible) necessary for a class of human beings to perform their economically defined roles. I talk about 'a class' rather than of 'individual members' of a class, because we must allow for the possibility that any one of innumerable special circumstances may allow an individual to occupy a given class position, for varying amounts of time, with less than the minimal model ideological formation required. All classes have their 'misfits'.

1. Class Ego-Ideologies

Let us then first examine the world that a child destined to become a (male) *feudal aristocrat* must be subjected to and qualified for.

(i) A feudal aristocrat has access to means of production in the form of a landed estate — characteristically enjoyed with individual family property rights (though other forms may develop) and assured through military prowess or other services to a supreme lord, and through inheritance and marriage. Ideologically, this implies a formation in which landed wealth, martialism, and bravery — and/or service, obligation, descent, and non-romantic marriage — are highly salient both in structuring conceptions of what the world is like and what is possible in it and in defining what is good and right.

(ii) The feudal lord occupies a position outside the day-to-day management of the means of production, which falls to his peasants under the supervision of his non-aristocratic bailiffs. He is related to fellow-aristocrats and to his king in a hierarchy defined in the non-economic, juridico-political terms of rights and powers, trust, pledge, and lineage. He is similarly related to direct producers, his peasants, though he is separated from them through the qualitative demarcation between aristocratic and non-aristocratic lineage. These aspects of the relations of production imply an ideological formation tailored to awareness and appreciation of legal hierarchy, command, honour, fidelity, and lineage.

(iii) Feudal production is oriented to appropriation of the surplus through lordly consumption. Its ideological counterpart is training for stylish consumption and comportment.

The world of the *feudal peasants*, by contrast, is first of all defined by the fact that they collectively belong to the land without owning it. The peasants are separated from ownership of the land and from the surplus produced upon it, and are subordinate to a lord as tillers of his estate. The subjection to and qualification for this historical form of social existence implies a collectivist orientation, and ideological attachment to one's native land and village, and an acquisition of agricultural skills that are traditional and slow-changing because of the slow pace of development of the feudal productive forces. Although the formation of feudal peasants does not extend to any political questions of state, it does include a consciousness and appreciation of legal rights and obligations: they are not human beasts of burden, but occupiers of the lowest rung of a legally-defined hierarchy of rights and obligations.

Now let us turn to the capitalist world of the *bourgeoisie*.

(i) A capitalist typically has access to means of production whose intrinsic character is irrelevant so long as they can be put to profitable use. This access can be gained through possession of liquid resources exchangeable on a competitive market; through inheritance; or, increasingly, through membership of a corporate executive and successful realization of profits in an employed capacity. Corresponding to this is an ideological formation that emphasizes the making of wealth, industry, initiative, and peaceful risk-taking, competitiveness, and individual achievement and mastery of nature.

(ii) The capitalist typically participates in the work process of his enterprise, running it on the basis of the subordination of manual to intellectual labour. He has to face his workers on a labour market, as a buyer of labour-power confronting legally free and equal sellers. His relation to other members of his class is one of competition and market-exchange. Given the goals of capitalist production, both relations are governed by the rule of profit and imply ideological training in a commodity conception of the world, in 'commodity fetishism'. Here the emphasis is on awareness and appreciation of juridical equality, of unequal rewards for unequal competitive performance, of the virtues of practical, enriching mental labour, and a consciousness of the prices of objects and men.

(iii) The institutionalized objective of capitalist production is the accumulation of capital — investment for profit in order to invest for further profit. This requires an ideological subjection to and qualification for rational calculation, orderliness, thrift, and continuous effort. And given the existential problem of the meaning of accumulation, it tends to be combined with a nuclear-family orientation that makes it possible to cope with continued accumulation and the transfer of property. Under corporate capitalism some of these requirements are met by corporate institutionalization such that thrift, the family, and so on, are no longer crucial in the ideological formation of individual capitalists.[28]

Petty-bourgeois ideology should be determined theoretically in the same manner. It should not, as is very often the case, simply be used as a catch-all category into which any modern ideology that is neither fully bourgeois nor fully revolutionary-proletarian can be consigned.[29] The petty-bourgeois world of simple commodity producers and traders is, like the bourgeois one, a world of markets and competition. But it involves no employees and no appropriation of surplus labour, and it is economically oriented to family consumption rather than capital accumulation. These differences seem to imply that indiscriminate bourgeois wealth-making, initiative, and risk-taking would here be replaced by ideologies according to which hard work and thrift govern access (and the maintenance of access) to the means of production; that superordinate mental labour would be replaced by the economic practicality of the single producer or trader; that the egalitarian component would be stronger and more material; and that considerations of family security and independence would take priority over rational calculation of profits. So-called professionals typically form part of the petty bourgeoisie as well — though many are in fact employed middle strata (e.g., public-sector doctors), and others are rather intellectual hangers-on of the high bourgeoisie (corporate lawyers, accountants, 'consultants'). A 'professional' orientation may be a variant of petty-bourgeois ideology, with its emphasis on independence and disinterested work ethic unrelated to consideration of profitability.

The world of the *working class* is one of individual and total separation from the means of production on the basis of non-possession of earned or inherited capital. A working-class existence carries *both* the legal freedom and equality of a market-subject owning undifferentiated labour-power, *and* the group-subordination that collectively interdependent manual workers experience in relation to managerial mental labour geared to the accumulation of surplus-value. The ideological formation of a worker involves first of all an orientation to work, to manual labour, including physical prowess, toughness, endurance, and dexterity. The wage-contract implies a distinction between work and leisure, the purpose of work being consumption and family reproduction. The capitalist work process further implies a collectivist awareness of interdependence. Finally, as legally free and equal market agents who are 'citizens' of a state, workers under capitalism differ from feudal peasants in that they are inherently open to *political* ideological formation.

Critical readers will undoubtedly detect a number of outstanding problems in this definition of class ideologies. Qualification, specification, and additions are clearly required. Though some hints in this direction were made above in relation to bourgeois ideology, it may be necessary, following the same kind of procedure, to make further points with reference to different stages in a mode of production and the existence of its classes. Class ideologies may also be made more specific according to the fractions in question. More generally, I do not claim that the list given above exhausts the central elements of class ideologies. On the contrary, one crucial missing component will be discussed below, and there may well be others. I do assert, however, subject to revision, that the list includes elements necessary to the ideological constitution of the classes involved.

The middle strata are not bearers of a particular mode of production but the product of a development of capitalism. Therefore they cannot constitute a class in the strict Marxist sense. Their position is probably best grasped by means of the concept of 'contradictory class location' developed by Erik Olin Wright.[30] Ideologically, then, they would also exhibit a contradictory class location: between the bourgeoisie, the working class, and the petty bourgeoisie.

It will have been noticed that although both the feudal peasant and the capitalist worker are exploited — that is, they perform surplus labour appropriated by others — acceptance of exploitation is not at all part of the definition of their respective class ideologies. To Marxists this omission may well seem quite reasonable, even though it may appear not to follow logically from the premises. On the other hand, no revolutionary elements have been included in the definition of the ideologies of the exploited classes; this is logically consistent with the argument itself, but it will appear strange and unreasonable to many Marxists.

The answer to these objections is as follows. Our symmetrical and deliberate omission of both acceptance of and resistance to exploitation is logically grounded in the fact that the determinations so far specified refer only to the *ego-ideologies* of the classes in question. However, we also said that all positional ideologies have a double character, since they include both an ego-ideology and a related *alter-ideology*. Ego-ideologies relate one subject (in this case one class) to another or to several others. It is these *class alter-ideologies* that *constitute the subjects of class struggle and class collaboration.*

2. Class Alter-Ideologies

These class alter-ideologies are not simply invented as deceptions or myths of struggle, but are inscribed in the relations of production, just like ego-ideologies. From the standpoint of the ideological constitution of class-struggle subjects, the crucial aspect of the alter-ideology is, in the case of exploiting classes, the rationale for their domination of other classes; in the case of exploited classes, it is the basis for their resistance to the exploiters.

Feudal relations of production thus seem to involve an *aristocratic alter-ideology* that centres on the following: inferior and superior *birth*; lineage and descent; the distinction between those born to rule (the aristocracy) and those born to work for them (the peasants); *inferior and superior service*, which, given the dynamics of feudal society, involved production, work, and trade, and armed protection, military, and legal statecraft respectively. The very existence of an ongoing feudal mode of production means, ideologically, that this aristocratic alter-ideology is in some way accepted by the peasantry, or is at least not actively questioned. However, the hierarchy of feudal society, including the exploitative nexus between a lord and his peasants, was defined in terms of an exchange of services and obligations. Here, I would argue, is the typical basis for feudal peasant resistance. Feudal peasants were not toiling non-persons but occupied a hierarchical position with some rights and (more) obligations. Rights and obligations, however, may be interpreted in varying ways, and entail a potential class experience that rights are being violated and obligations overstretched. *Peasant alter-ideology* therefore involved conceptions of 'just' rights and obligations, and it was around these rights and obligations that the feudal class struggle revolved.[31]

Bourgeois alter-ideology, set against the capitalist channels of access to means of production and the capitalist orientation of production, exhibits the notion that non-market enterprise is of inherently lesser economic rationality, and that inferior individual performance results in lack of success in attaining positions of power and wealth. Since, legally speaking, equal opportunities exist for all, workers have only themselves to blame for being workers, for not having worked and saved hard enough, for not being clever enough. Attacks on capitalism are economically irrational, and have a negative effect on the material well-being of all. The existence of capitalism as a going concern implies that this bourgeois alter-ideology is accepted by the workers, whether actively or passively, consciously or unconsciously. (In relation to the feudal aristocracy, bourgeois alter-ideology centres on the superiority of rational productive — mental — labour over the economic idleness and irrational *sans-souciance* of the aristocrat.)

Proletarian alter-ideology starts from the buying and selling of labour-power on the market. In this context, the owners of labour-power stand in a peculiar situation, which provides the basis for their alter-ideology in all its aspects. On the one hand, they are individual market-agents, free and equal in relation to the purchasers of labour-power. On the other hand, they also constitute a separate class (in the logical sense) of market agents, having only a very special commodity to trade, their labour-power, which is an inseparable part of human capacity. Inherent in this situation seems to be resistance to the total conversion of labour-power into a commodity: an assertion of the *working person*, with rights to employment, adequate subsistence and some degree of security, counterposed to the commodity-rationality of the market and of capital accumulation. This is further strengthened by direct involvement in the labour process, as distinct from the profit-making activities of the entrepreneur/manager.

The bargaining situation of workers is so structured that their strength does not depend (primarily) on the commodity they are trading — which has little individual specificity — nor on their individual capacity to 'see out' the purchaser of their commodity. Rather it derives from their great numerical superiority over the capitalists — provided, of course, that they can effectively come together. Another central aspect of proletarian ideology, then, is *solidarity*, as opposed to competitive individualism. Trade unions are the most characteristic and universal of working-class institutions.

Further, the dual labour-market situation tends to generate *class consciousness*, in the sense of an awareness of economic differentiation and conflict between whole categories or 'classes' as distinct from legally free and equal market-subjects. This awareness also involves a tendency to class political action, since workers as a class of free and equal market-subjects are also free and equal members or 'citizens' of a state. Working-class parties are also a near-universal phenomenon in developed capitalist societies.

The alter-ideologies of resistance peculiar to dominated and exploited classes are inscribed in the kind of subjection-qualification that constitutes the exploited subjects of a given mode of production. Thus, the feudal subjection of peasants to a number of obligations simultaneously qualifies them not only to carry out those obligations but also to gain an awareness of certain rights and a capacity to assert them. Capitalism subjects workers to commodity relations and the rationality of capital accumulation, yet it qualifies them not only to produce surplus-value but also to act and bargain as free persons.

The alter-, as well as the ego-ideologies, actually develop, with the mode of production itself, in social processes of ideological interpellation and through a learning process governed by various forms of affirmations and sanctions. This ideological development involves both a series of individual processes, in childhood as well as in adult life, and processes of collective formation and collective organization. The latter range from princely courts, setting the tone for aristocratic codes of conduct, and peasant village communities, via burgher councils and business associations to factories, mutual aid societies and trade unions.

The ideological constitution of new classes, of course, always takes place on the basis of pre-existing ideologies and economic and political conditions, which always assume unique historical forms in different societies. Proletarian alter-ideology, for instance, was able to draw upon previous peasant and artisan ideology in resisting the march of capitalist commodity-relations. But the sanction of defeat compelled the working class-in-formation to abandon peasant and artisan solutions to its proletarianization. It also had to confront and overcome bourgeois ideologies — those that centred on the united 'industrial' or 'productive class', on individual self-education and self-improvement, and on the spread of 'reason', all lavishly diffused but gradually proving to be inadequate to the situation of workers under capitalism.

It will no doubt have been observed, and doubtless with alarm by some, that these central aspects of the alter-ideology of dominated classes, while they constitute subjects of class struggle, do not explicitly point to the transcendence of the given mode of exploitation and domination. I have deliberately not included 'socialism', not to speak of Marxism or Marxism-Leninism, in working-class alter-ideology. The reason for this scandalous omission is that classes and class struggle are, in Marxist theory, constitutive of the functioning of exploitative modes of production. Hence, the class struggle in itself does not transcend the mode of exploitation and domination on which it is based and in which it operates. What leads to social revolution is the contradictory and disarticulating dynamic of a given mode of production; such a revolution is the product of class struggle under changed parameters resulting from that very dynamic. The class struggle is part of the ongoing reproduction of a given mode of production, as well as the motive force of its transformation. The contradictory and disarticulating dynamic does not necessarily originate in the existing nexus of exploitation. Capitalism did not develop out of the lord-peasant nexus, but in the interstices of feudalism, though it is true that the bourgeois revolution was also linked to peasant struggles. The transition from capitalism to socialism, of course, was posited by Marx as growing directly out of the capital-labour relation, but only because the terrain of the capital-labour conflict changes with the development of capitalism.[32]

In my estimation, it cannot be logically argued that a socialist ideology — an ideology according to which a socialist society is both good and possible to achieve — is implicit in working-class existence and therefore forms part of working-class ideology. Kautsky and Lenin were in this sense correct in their view of the difference between working-class and socialist ideology. It is, of course, a fact that the main social force of socialist (and communist) ideology has been and is the working class. But it is possible to account for this without either including socialism in working-class ideology, or having recourse to the dubious utilitarian notion of 'interest'. Between working-class and socialist ideology there is a strong *selective affinity*, a potentiality for mutual linkage and articulation, which exists between socialism and no other class ideology. Socialism is, in fact, a projection into a future society, and a specification within a political strategy, of all the central elements of working-class ideology: its collectivist orientation to productive labour, its affirmation of the working person over and against commodity relations, its class consciousness and solidarity. A similar special affinity exists between working-class ideology and Marxist theory, between proletarian class consciousness and the Marxist propositions about the overriding importance of class relations and struggle in capitalist society over and against those of individual competitive performance. Marxist socialism also comprises a theory of the particular capacities and potentialities of the working class, focusing on its position in the contradictory development of capitalism. And in this last respect, Marxism adds a strategic direction to working-class struggle.

Now, given the way working-class ideology has been defined and determined, this is tantamount to saying that socialist ideology and Marxist theory have a bond of affinity with working-class existence. It is not just a question of an encounter in the realm of ideologies. Moreover, Marxist socialism was not just a creation of intellectuals. It developed through what Marx and Engels learned from the working class and its struggles.[33]

3. Class and Non-Class Ideologies

Thinking still of some likely criticisms of our analysis, we should next discuss the articulation of class ideologies with existential- and historical-inclusive ideologies. This is indeed a central problem for a Marxist theory of ideology, because historical materialism asserts that these ideologies and forms of subjectivity are articulated with different classes in different ways. In the interests of space, I will limit myself to a few brief remarks.

First, it is noteworthy that feudal and bourgeois ego-ideologies have been very strongly gender-specific, most of their specific aspects pertaining only to male members of the class. (Faced with a choice, I have considered the ideological constitution of feudal and bourgeois males, since it was typically they alone who were *directly* involved in the extraction and appropriation of surplus labour.) This is much less true of working-class ideology — in fact, gender-specificity there pertains only, in a varying degree, to the element of physical toughness. Here may be seen one of the main reasons for the historical links, however difficult, between the labour and women's movements. (Since class ideology does not exhaust the ideological make-up of the members of a class, this does *not* mean that blatant male sexism has not existed and does not exist among the working class.) The reasons for the greater gender-specificity of feudal and capitalist ideologies probably has much to do with the role of the family in regulating the transfer of property, with the military orientation of feudalism, and with the great importance of physical strength in its characteristic forms of warfare. With the development of corporate capitalism, where capital becomes separated from the family, a lesser degree of gender-specificity should be expected in bourgeois ego-ideology. Indeed, the role of the family appears to be a key to the degree of gender-specificity of class ideologies. Peasant labour and subjectivity were gender-specific within the family production-unit. Gender differences were accentuated when the family was dissociated from production, taking on the specialized role of regulating descent and property. The family had little relevance to the exploitation of slaves and workers, and plantation-slavery and early industrial capitalism entailed relatively little gender-specificity in their direct producers. The later reassertion of the working-class family should perhaps be seen as the combined effect of bourgeois ego-ideology and working-class resistance to commodification.

Second, something must be said about religion, for it is historical fact that the Church was a central ideological apparatus in feudal Europe. Given the level of the productive forces and of knowledge about nature, we should expect supranaturalist existential ideologies about the meaning of life and death to have played an important role in human life, a role enhanced by the massive suffering caused by war, pestilence, natural disasters, and the ordinary scarcity afflicting most men and women in feudal society. We might even find a selective affinity between a class ideology stressing inborn social distinctions and a religion offering life after death. In fact, the need for religion as a device to contain the exploited masses was explicitly stated by a host of feudal ideologists. That said, however, it must also be pointed out that no theory of feudalism and feudal classes can explain either the core of prevailing religious doctrine or the position of the Church. And the fact that the Catholic Church played an important role as opponent and target of the European bourgeois revolutions does not make it an intrinsically feudal institution (as we know, it both predated and postdates feudalism). All we can conclude is that, in crucial ways, it was institutionally linked to and ideologically articulated with the feudal organization of power.

Classes always exist in states, and for purposes of political analysis, the most important historical-inclusive ideology is that which addresses all members of the state. Under the feudal system, monarchism in the narrow sense of the term was precisely such an inclusive ideology, interpellating all 'subjects' of the monarchy. With the bourgeois revolution nationalism came to play a similar role, and socialist states also have often had recourse to this ideology. Now, the historical association of nationalism with the bourgeois revolution and bourgeois rule is, in some respects, rather puzzling. For there is not at all the same affinity between bourgeois class ideology and nationalism as there is between socialism and working-class ideology. Market rationality and competitive individualism have rather more in common with cosmopolitanism, which has also been characteristic of sections of the bourgeoisie, particularly its topmost echelons. Nationalism became linked to the bourgeois revolution by providing an ideology of struggle that counterposed to the dynastic and/or colonial power a state of legally free and equal citizens encompassing a certain territory. In the classical cases, the bourgeoisie was then able to lead and emerge as the victor of a vast and complex revolutionary process. However, if we are to probe a little further into the role of nationalism in established bourgeois rule, we must examine rather more deeply the character of inclusive historical ideologies.

Inclusive historical ideologies are not simply invented as formulae of ruling-class legitimation. Like the state itself, they express the historical outcome of struggles within and of the state. In their varying concrete forms they are expressions or repositories of the experiences and memories of a class-structured population. They thus have a dual character, expressing both a historical tradition of struggle (of which the popular classes are an important part) and the outcome of these struggles, which, by definition, has usually been a victory for the ruling class. They are repositories of struggles both for popular sovereignty and independence and against other peoples for territory, social position, and cultural rights. Since nationalism played a crucial role in the bourgeoisie's rise to power, it is quite natural that nationalism as an inclusive ideology, irreducible to class, should be articulated with the rule of the bourgeoisie.

However, it is also natural that subordinate classes should try to link up with the inclusive ideology, since its very inclusiveness means that it can be brought to bear upon members and sections of the ruling class. This may be done in one of two ways. The subordinate classes can relate to that dominant tendency of the inclusive historical ideology which expresses the outcome of historical struggles — witness the feudal peasants' appeals to the monarch or the rallying to the 'national cause' in 1914 by most of the working-class parties of the Second International. Or else they can relate to the popular struggles that also form part of the tradition of a state and are inscribed in its historical ideology. The anti-fascist Resistance and anti-imperialist liberation movements exemplify this latter kind of articulation. In other words, starting from the ideology of a subordinate class, one can either join the cause of the victors, embracing and subordinating oneself to the nationalist cause, or relate to the tradition of struggle, linking up with the 'national-popular' tradition.

Before we leave the inclusive historical ideologies, it should be pointed out that the history and present reality of a given state normally involve more than two classes, as well as a number of distinct strata. Hence, a class movement explicitly relating to national-popular traditions must also relate to the struggles of other popular classes. In the case of the labour movement under capitalism, this usually means the struggles of the peasantry and the petty bourgeoisie.

Class ideologies always have to compete with and relate to other positional ideologies. Only in working-class ideology does an element of class consciousness seem to be an intrinsic feature — although the feudal aristocracy, of course, had a very clear consciousness of the line of demarcation between noble and non-noble. However, this does not imply that class cohesiveness is necessarily greater in the proletariat than in other classes. Also to be considered are the logistics of class cohesion and the facilities for travel and communication, which invariably favour the leading sections of the ruling class. The main positional ideologies with which a given class ideology must compete in attempting to constitute united class subjects will differ considerably depending on the class in question. As far as the feudal aristocracy, the bourgeoisie, and the petty bourgeoisie are concerned, the most significant element of division is inherent in the class ideology itself: in the case of the aristocracy it is the salience of lineage; in the case of the bourgeoisie and petty bourgeoisie, it is the role played in transferring property by the individual (the subject of competitive individualism) and by the nuclear family. Working-class ideology, to assert itself, must above all confront and absorb occupational ideologies — the particular work-orientation and solidarity of particular occupations and crafts. In actual working-class history there is also the massive fact of migration, and the resulting phenomenon of multi-ethnic working classes, to which Marxists have devoted virtually no systematic attention. Given a multi-ethnic labour force, of course, ethnicity becomes a positional ideology competing with working-class ideology.

It has been argued above that the ideological universe is irreducible to class ideologies, but that the ideological ensemble of a class society is class-patterned and that ideological change is overdetermined by the class struggle. The thesis concerning the class patterning of ideologies is not dependent on any notion of 'representation'. Class ideologies, like class politics do not 'represent' anything other than themselves, such as 'class interests'. Indeed, the notion of 'representation' is part of the utilitarian heritage in Marxism, which should be definitely discarded. Class patterning refers to two different phenomena. First, the empirically observable fact that a given kind of ideological theme is differently related to the modes of existence of different classes and thereby tends to be more or less reformulated along class lines. Second, that for human beings to be able to act as subjects-incumbents of specific class positions they have to be formed as class subjects by class ideologies, analytically defined on the basis of the relations of production. These class ideologies then exist in various kinds of articulation with non-class ideologies.

4. Elaborations and Permutations of Class Ideologies

Class ideologies in the sense defined above are not doctrines or elaborated forms of discourse. They are rather class-specific *core themes* of discourse that vary enormously in concrete form and degree of elaboration. These core themes are the ideological counterpart of the social force and non-discursive practices of classes. And intellectuals, specialists in discursive practice, are institutionally linked to social classes, however great the 'relative autonomy' of their subjection-qualification.

The formation of specialist groups and strata of intellectuals is an aspect of a social division of labour broader than that implied in the relations of production. Their intellectual formation pertains to the whole universe of ideologies, which cannot be simply reduced to the realm of class ideologies. Particularly important is their relation to inclusive existential ideologies, religion and secular philosophy, and to the inclusive historical ideologies bound up with the state. However, the formation of such intellectuals is overdetermined by the form and amount of the appropriation of surplus labour — a process that provides the material basis of intellectual institutions, determines the basic social forces to which intellectuals must relate, and, in the case of state intellectuals, largely prescribes their tasks as part of the class-specific tasks of class-specific states. These existential- and historical-inclusive intellectuals Gramsci called 'traditional' intellectuals.[34]

Gramsci distinguished these from intellectuals organically linked to class-specific practices, the specialists and elaborators of class ideologies. Liberal economic and political writers, business lawyers, technicians, advertising specialists, bourgeois politicians and journalists are examples of 'organic' intellectuals of the bourgeoisie. The working class, too, has produced its own intellectuals: its orators, organizers, pamphlet-and song-writers, journalists, teachers at trade-union and party schools, and so on. The distinction being made here corresponds to Gramsci's, but it rests on a different basis — on the one hand, the specialized producers, elaborators and diffusers of existential- and historical-inclusive ideologies variously articulated with different classes; on the other hand, those devoted to specific class ideologies.

The development and struggle of classes both involves the production of organic class intellectuals and serves to restructure and realign the traditional intelligentsia. In some circumstances, certain members or sectors of this intelligentsia may come to abandon old class bonds and forge links with a new class. The rallying of Marx and Engels to the labour movement is a famous example of this process. Now, as I have shown in some detail elsewhere, this is not a unilateral gesture whereby cultured intellectuals bring light to the masses, as the Kautskyist conception tends to suggest, but is a complex two-way process of learning and unlearning.[35] Class ideologies, in innumerable ways, develop, undergo elaboration, compete, clash, and are affected by other discourses, including those of other classes. This takes place around their specific core themes, through the work of intellectuals in constant interaction with class practices, and within historical modes of signifying production. To be sure, the role of intellectuals, in the broad Gramscian sense, is not confined to the elaboration of ideology. Equally important is their role in setting ideologies against one another, sharpening and clarifying differences, and thereby developing and intensifying commitment to certain ideologies. We shall return below to questions concerning ideological mobilization.

IV
The Social Order
of Ideologies

1. The Social Process of Ideology

Having set out some general propositions about the dialectical operation, material determination and class structuring of ideology, we will now look more concretely at the functioning of ideologies, particularly in contemporary capitalist societies. In order to reach an understanding of the social order and of ideology, particularly in contemporary advanced capitalist societies, we must first grasp that ideologies actually operate in a state of *disorder* compared with the conception traditional in the history of ideas. Ideologies function neither as bodies of thought that we possess and invest in our actions, nor as elaborate texts presenting the thought of great minds, which other minds then examine, memorize, accept or reject, like visitors passing the exhibits in a museum. To understand how ideologies operate in a given society requires first of all that we see them not as possessions or texts but as *ongoing social processes*. It is precisely as such processes that they interpellate or address us; and the rarest form of interpellation is the one implicit in the traditional historiography of ideas, namely, an elaborate written text speaking directly to a solitary reader.

As ongoing social processes, then, ideologies are not

possessions. They do not constitute 'states of mind', above all because the ideological interpellations unceasingly constitute and reconstitute who we are. A single human being may act as an almost unlimited number of subjects, and in the course of a single human life a large number of subjectivities are in fact acted out. In any situation, particularly in a complex modern society, a given human being usually has several subjectivities that might be applied, although as a rule only one at a time. Ideologies differ, compete, and clash not only in what they say about the world we inhabit, but also in telling us who we are, in the kind of subject they interpellate. And these different interpellations of what exists are usually connected with different interpellations of what is right and what is possible for such a subject.

For example, when a strike is called, a worker may be addressed as a member of the working class, as a union member, as a mate of his fellow workers, as the long-faithful employee of a good employer, as a father or mother, as an honest worker, as a good citizen, as a Communist or an anti-communist, as a Catholic, and so on. The kind of address accepted — 'Yes, that's how I am, that's me!' — has implications for how one acts in response to the strike call. The ideological struggle is not fought out solely between competing world-views. It is also a struggle over the assertion of a particular subjectivity — for example, as an individual believer, citizen, or member of a class; over the definition of (the inclusion in, or exclusion from) particular subjects like 'the productive classes', the 'people', or the 'exploited'; and over which subjectivity should apply, as in the example of a strike call.

The statement that ideologies interpellate subjects means that the former are not received as something external by a fixed and unified subject. To the extent that a particular interpellation is received, the receiver changes and is (re)constituted. The often-noted contrast between, on the one hand, expressions of acquiescence and satisfaction, and on the other, sudden outbursts of revolt, is only a dramatic, special instance of this general phenomenon. As he or she is the target of constant conflicting or simply competing interpellations, the receiver is not necessarily consistent in his or her receptions and responding acts and interpellations. Moreover, the psychic structure underlying our conscious subjectivities is not monolithic either, but rather a field of conflicting forces. Even more important, however, is the fact that the ideological (re)formation of subjectivities is a social process. The sudden shifts between acquiescence and revolt are collective processes, not merely a series of individual changes. These collective processes are largely governed by openings and closures in the existing power matrix of affirmations and sanctions — openings and closures that may be quite insignificant at first but then may rapidly become decisive, through the collective dynamics of counter-power or powerlessness.

It is not only the interpellated or interpellating subjects that have no fixed unity and consistency. Ideologies themselves are equally protean. For analytic purposes different ideologies may be identified according to their source, topic, content, or interpellated subject. But as ongoing processes of interpellation, they have no natural boundaries, no natural criteria distinguishing one ideology from another or one element of an ideology from its totality. Particularly in today's open and complex societies, different ideologies, however defined, not only coexist, compete, and clash, but also overlap, affect, and contaminate one another. This holds for relations both between class ideologies and between class and non-class ideologies. A class ideology exists in self-contained purity only as an analytical construct, and, in elaborated form, possibly as a doctrinal text. Further, ideologies do not operate as immaterial ideas or interpellations. They are always produced, conveyed, and received in particular, materially circumscribed social situations and through special means and practices of communication, the material specificity of which bears upon the efficacy of a given ideology. Technology affects the range of possible communication, and its cost affects the distribution of the available means of communication. Yet the technology and ecology of communication tend to have an effect upon ideological relations of force, regardless of ownership. The outwardly closed and internally dense and intricate network of a study group, or of the meeting of an organization, tends to create a relatively stable, collective effect different from the momentous impact of a loud-speaker address on a mass audience, or from the individualized effect inherent in a television speech received at home, even if it is class interpellations that are being televised.

Let us end this section by briefly examining some aspects of how ideological battles are waged, won, and lost — even if we cannot offer a manual on 'how to win an ideological argument'. The stakes of an ideological battle are either the reconstitution, desubjection-resubjection and requalification of already-constituted subjects, or their reproduction in the face of a challenge. In this process there are four kinds of problem to be solved. First, the speaker or 'agitator' has to establish his or her right to speak to, and to be given a hearing by the subjects addressed, as being one of them or as having a position and a kind of knowledge that somehow fits into their conception of what should command respect. Second, he or she must assert the overriding relevance of a particular kind of identity, say that of 'workers' as opposed to 'Christians', 'Englishmen', or 'football fans'. This mode of interpellation therefore implies the assertion that certain features of the world are more important than others — for example, exploitation rather than interdependence or affluence. This is done by referring and relating to certain experiences of the interpellees, either present or past. Third, interpellations of what is good and bad must be situated in relation to elements of the prevailing normative conceptions. Thus it may be argued, following a logical thread connected to prevailing conceptions, that the new and changed circumstances require certain new norms to be accepted. Finally, the call to some kind of action implies that the proposed course is the only or the best possible way to achieve the normative goals. And this again requires that the speaker relate to existing experiences. Alternatively, it may be necessary to affirm a normative principle according to which a certain course of action is an ethical necessity regardless of the possibility of success. This ideological battle is always fought in a matrix of non-discursive affirmations and sanctions, past and present, with a particular set of means and in a particular ecological setting of communication.

What has been said here is, of course, very general. But at least it should suffice to demonstrate that winning an ideological struggle, or a struggle for hegemony, involves much more than just having the 'right programme', making the 'right interpellations', or providing the 'correct leadership'.

2. The Social Organization of Ideological Discourse

Although the operation of ideologies cannot be reduced to the neat textual unities with which the historian of ideas is concerned, or to the outstanding themes that fascinate or anger cultural critics, there is nevertheless in every society an ideological order of power, control, and domination. We have conceived of ideology as operating through discursive practices inscribed in matrices of non-discursive practices (or, more precisely, as practices whose discursive dimension is dominant, inscribed in practices in which the non-discursive dimension dominates). From this it follows that there are two components of the organization of ideological domination. One is the construction and maintenance of a particular order of discourse. The other involves the deployment of non-discursive affirmations and sanctions.

The construction of a discursive order in a particular society is the historical outcome of struggles waged by social forces at crucial moments of contradiction and crisis. According to historical materialism, the decisive aspect of these struggles in class societies is the class struggle, and the resulting discursive order is a class order, articulated with existential- and historical-inclusive discourses. The maintenance of a given discursive order involves, in its predominantly discursive dimension, the production and reproduction of discursive affirmations and sanctions and of a particular structuring of social discourse.

The discursive affirmation of a given ideology or ideological order is organized through affirmative symbolism or *ritual*, from the Christian holy communion and the waving of the national flag to the singing of the Internationale. The distinction between a ritual and a material affirmation is an analytical one and not a distinction between intrinsically ritual and non-ritual practices. A political election in a capitalist state, for instance, is an affirmation of liberal political ideology. To the extent that the outcome is predetermined by limits on who may run and have a chance to campaign effectively, or by outright rigging of the vote, the affirmation is predominantly ritual. But to the extent that the outcome is open we should regard the affirmation as predominantly material.

The (predominantly) discursive form of sanction is a limiting type of interpellation, which negates subjectivity by turning the interpellee into an object. This is *excommunica-*

tion, the victim of which is excluded from further meaningful discourse as being insane, depraved, traitorous, alien, and so on. The excommunicated person is condemned, temporarily or forever, to ideological non-existence: he is not to be listened to; he is the target of ideological objectification; he is someone whose utterances are to be treated only as symptoms of something else, of insanity, depravity, and the like. Usually, ideological excommunication is connected with the material sanctions of expulsion, confinement, or death.

In his discussion of the structuring of discourse, Foucault has drawn up a perceptive catalogue of procedures used for the control, selection, organization, and redistribution of discourse, procedures which he groups under the three main types of exclusion, limitation, and appropriation.[35] Without critically examining the specific features of Foucault's analytical approach, we may use these three categories to sum up the social organization of discourse. But although we cannot discuss Foucault's problematic, perhaps we ought to reformulate these procedures in a more general terminology. We shall therefore designate them as the restriction, the shielding, and the delimited appropriation of discourse.

The *restriction* of discourse refers to socially institutionalized restrictions on who may speak, how much may be said, what may be talked about, and on what occasion. These kinds of restriction occur in every society, in various forms and extensions, and are not at all dependent on state institutions of censorship. They operate first of all through asserted definitions and patterns of subjectivity, buttressed by excommunication and material sanctions and by the distribution of the means of communication. The existing order of ideologically constituted subjectivity implies that, in a given situation, only persons of a certain age, sex, knowledge, social position and so on are allowed to speak (or will be listened to), about a set range of topics for a set length of time.

The *shielding* of discourse refers to procedures internal to a given discourse which are designed to protect it from other discourses which (are allowed to) exist. One such procedure is author-ization. This establishes the principle that one author — be he God (supposedly the true author of the ghost-written Bible and Koran), Marx, or someone else — or certain authors or a particular type of author are the only (or the main) ones who can make valid assertions. Another procedure is to ensure the incessant repetition of a given discourse, such that the only valid enunciations apart from the authorized text itself are exegesis, commentary, and reinterpretation. There is also a more global form of protecting a given discourse which consists in organizing it as a discipline with an institutionalized domain of enunciations, methods, propositions, and set rules. 'Politics' may be turned into a discipline in this sense, as the revolutionary labour movement and the feminist movement have revealed in their (differing and often mutually conflictual) responses to male-bourgeois political discourse and practice.

The structuring of the discursive order further involves the *delimited appropriation of discourse*, whereby its reception is restrictively situated. For instance, religious discourse, 'education', political speeches and discussions are situated in determinate ecological settings: in churches, schools, and special periods and sites of political campaigning. This social organization of discourse is circumscribed by predominantly non-discursive affirmation-recognition, and by the sanctions of confinement, violence, death, fines, unemployment, bankruptcy, starvation, and so on.

3. Ideological Apparatuses

Ideological interpellations are made all the time, everywhere and by everybody. They always have a non-discursive, material aspect, but it hardly makes sense to say that ideologies exist only in apparatuses, as Althusser has argued, unless the word 'apparatus' is emptied of all institutional meaning. Even less seems to be gained from calling the institutional matrices of ideologies 'state apparatuses'. Many of the apparatuses mentioned by Althusser, such as the family, do not at all form part of the state in the ordinary sense of the word. It seems rather sterile and even actively confusing, from an analytical point of view, to extend the concept of the state to cover everything that serves the reproduction of a social order. Moreover, it goes against the Marxist concept of the state as a special organization, separate from the rest of society and bound up with the existence of classes. Althusser himself is no longer prepared to defend the theoretical necessity of the notion 'ideological state apparatus', maintaining that the crucial point is to grasp the intrinsic link between the ideological apparatuses and the state (in the usual sense of the term).[36] This, in my opinion, is both a correct and an important way of posing the question. The ideological apparatuses are part of the organization of power in society, and the social relations of power are condensed and crystallized within the state. The family, for example, is regulated by state legislation and jurisdiction, and affected by the forms of maleness and femaleness, sexual union, parenthood and childhood that are prescribed, favoured, or permitted by the state.

However, even though ideological interpellations occur everywhere, both discourses and their protecting mechanisms of restriction, shielding, and delimited appropriation — together with the related affirmations, sanctions, rituals, and excommunications — tend to cluster at those nodal points in the societal process which we may call *ideological apparatuses*. These apparatuses are settings of clustered discourse and related non-discursive practices, and settings or sites of ideological conflict. The social organization of discourse entails that a set of ideological apparatuses be structured in a particular way into a system of linkages and interdependence.

We may illustrate the system of ideological apparatuses by a simple model of the formation of class members in contemporary advanced capitalist society (Figure 1). If we assume, for the purposes of simplicity and manageability, that the pattern and maintenance of class roles or places are given, then the reproductive problem of the social order is to subject and qualify the infants of a new generation such that the places are filled in given proportions by subjects with skills adequate for each (type of) role. In terms of class ideology this involves, above all, two processes: (a) the inculcation of ruling-class ego-ideology (through ruling-class families and schools, and so on) into new members born into the class and into any outsiders permitted to enter; and (b) the teaching of future members of the ruled classes the dominance of ruling-class alter-ideology over the ideology of the ruled classes (in which the legislative and judicial power of the state, backed by forces of repression, usually plays an essential part). This subjection-qualification is realized in a system of interrelated ideological apparatuses. All such apparatuses are traversed by the class struggle, but even in a simplified model we should make a distinction between two types of apparatus bearing upon the formation of class members. One is *predominantly* a manifestation of the ruling-class (or ruling alliance's) organization of power and discourse; the other is made up of what we might call *counter-apparatuses*, which largely express, although in varying degree, the resistance and discourse of the ruled classes.

This model is purely descriptive; it is intended to show the elements of new class-member formation and the way

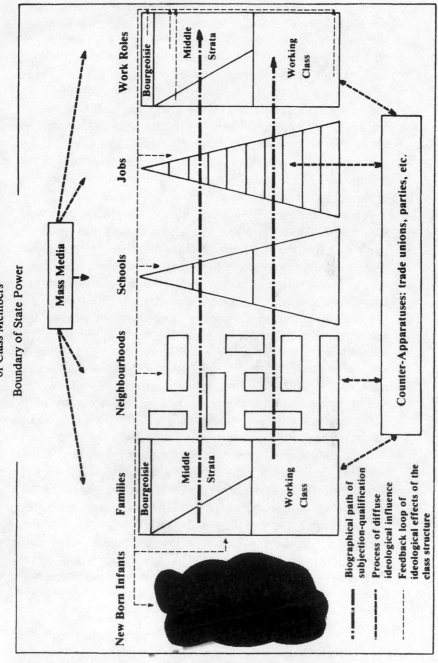

Figure 1

ideological apparatuses are interconnected in this process. It also brings out very clearly the severe limitations of the liberal concern with mobility — that is, with the question of whether individual biographical paths are straight (no mobility) or bent upwards or downwards. None of this affects the class structure, to the far right in the figure. What the rate of mobility does affect, however, is the power of bourgeois ideology, whose competitive individualism is materially affirmed by the mobility paths. In this sense, the great interest of bourgeois sociology in social mobility may be seen as a concern with one significant aspect of bourgeois domination.

A few additional remarks about the simplifications built into the model are required. It is assumed here that gender is irrelevant to the formation of class members, although we have already emphasized that this is not the case. Many women, particularly in the bourgeoisie, are formed to become wives of male members of their class. In practice, the ideological apparatuses do not constitute an irreversible sequence, as may be seen from the figure. They are normally entered in the sequence indicated above, but the formative effects of 'earlier' stages will usually sustain themselves alongside the 'new' effects of 'later' ones.

The figure may easily suggest an unrealistic neatness of fit between the formative apparatuses and the class structure. In fact, the class structure itself is not static, and every generational cohort contains its formative failures. More-over, the way in which the model incorporates the feedback loop from the class structure to the ideological apparatuses and the demographic pattern, and the representation of the counter-apparatuses of the ruled classes only very feebly and abstractly convey the complexities involved in expanded reproduction and class struggle. Another important aspect that is very difficult to convey figuratively is the inherently ambiguous role of the working-class family, neighbourhood and workplace. In an ongoing process of capitalist reproduction the working-class ego-ideology generated and diffused in them is, by definition, intertwined with the inculcation of bourgeois alter-ideology. However, they are at the same time producers and diffusers of working-class alter-ideology, and, to varying extents, sites of resistance. The model tries to portray this by drawing lines of ideological influence going in both directions between working-class families, neighbourhoods and workplaces, on one hand, and the separate ideological counter-apparatuses of the organized labour movement.

Finally, the model does not rank the apparatuses in terms of their relative weight and importance. This seems to vary considerably from country to country, and a sceptical stance towards the assertion by several French Marxists of the Althusserian tradition, that the school system is *the* most important ideological apparatus of (contemporary) capitalism, seems warranted. For instance, the relative weight of the schools in relation to on-the-job training and workplace hierarchies of seniority varies significantly across the geography and history of capitalism. So does the importance of the neighbourhood, in relation to, say, the mass media. It was much greater in the classical working-class communities prior to the Second World War than it is today. It is stronger in multi-ethnic or communalist societies than in those more homogenous in this respect. And neighbourhoods are more important in the *quartiers* of the Latin countries with their old local public institutions of cafés, street life and markets, than in the Germanic or Anglo-Saxon countries.

V
Ideology
and Political Power

This chapter will explore the role of ideology in the organization and maintenance of political power. It will address itself directly to some central problems in political theory, by developing a critique of and an alternative to the classical and still prevailing problematics of force/consent, legitimacy, and true and mystified consciousness.

1. Forms of Ideological Domination

The model presented in Figure 1 outlined the contours of the organization of an ideological system, but it did not treat the ideological *mechanisms of subjection*, which ensure that the rule of the ruling class is obeyed by the ruled. It is to this that we will turn now.

The ideological rapport that binds the population to a given regime, as the latter's obedient subjects, is essentially very complex and, of course, exhibits wide empirical variation. Nevertheless, it seems possible to identify the main types of the mechanism by the effects of domination and obedience they produce.

The typological axes are, first, the three modes of interpellation we identified earlier, centring on what exists, what is good and what is possible. This dimension refers to

93

the *present* situation, to the ways in which it is (predominantly) talked and thought about. The second dimension, on the other hand, refers to conceptions of the *absent*. Here the modes of interpellation have been collapsed and then dichotomized in terms of the answer to the question: Does there exist a possible better alternative to the present regime? Yes or No? The rationale for this second axis is that there is an important difference between obedience as an intrinsic necessity (or an intrinsically rational choice) and obedience based on contingent considerations.

Mechanisms of Subjection by their Effect of Ideological Domination

Mode of interpellation	Alternative regime conceivable	
	Yes	No
What is	*Accommodation*	*Sense of inevitability*
What is good	*Sense of representation*	*Deference*
What is possible	*Fear*	*Resignation*

Any value this typology may have does not derive from a classificatory function, and in any event it is not intended to fulfil the tasks of classification. Such a procedure never takes one very far on the road to understanding, and in this case it would be rather beside the point, since the mechanisms tend to be empirically intertwined with one another. Rather, it is proposed as an analytical tool that is both theoretically systematic (as opposed to *ad hoc* and intuitive) and sufficiently complex: it offers a way out of the constrictive dichotomy of force and consent, and the rationalist-idealist traditions of 'legitimacy' or 'false consciousness'.

These six types of ideological domination all operate in contemporary bourgeois-democratic societies, although their relative importance varies with the country and the time. A strategy for social transformation and revolution will therefore have to combat all these forms. The terms used to designate the six effects of domination largely speak for themselves, but they may need some further clarification.

Accommodation refers to a kind of acquiescence in which the rulers are obeyed because the ruled are constituted to regard other features in the world as more salient to them than both their present subordination and the possibility of an alternative regime. Among such features we may mention work-performance (regardless of exploitation), leisure, consumption, the family, sex, and sport. These are all central aspects of human activity, and accommodation is probably the most common form by far of dominated acquiescence. Accommodation may be seen to be brought about by a particular social distribution of knowledge and ignorance. The oppressive and exploitative features of the present are kept in shadow, while opportunities are spotlit. The visibility of this play of light and shadow is, however, dependent on the presence of the appropriate affirmations and sanctions.

Accommodation also includes the possibility of accommodating opposition. There may be certain aspects of the existing regime that people are prepared to meet with opposition and disobedience, but that they do not systematically combat to the extent that their relevant demands are satisfied. Such accommodating opposition ranges from male working-class company unionism to non-class-conscious ethnic assertiveness and 'apolitical' feminism.

The sense of *inevitability* refers, of course, to obedience through ignorance of any alternative. It would be a mistake to think of this as merely a pre-modern phenomenon of fatalism. Rather, it is a component in the political marginalization of large sectors of the population in contemporary advanced capitalist societies. The United States, in particular, has produced an extraordinarily wide degree of marginalization, to the point where only half the population votes in presidential elections, and much fewer in other elections. Political marginalization implies exteriorization from the political system, which is seen as impossible to change yet not accorded any attributes of goodness or rightfulness. Marginalization seems often to be accompanied by a cynically critical view of the rulers.

When the rulers are obeyed because they are seen as ruling on behalf of the ruled, and because this situation is seen as good, then we may talk of obedience based on a *sense of representation*. It may be objected that it is misleading to call this an effect of ideological domination, and that I am allowing the previously discarded notion of 'false consciousness' to slip back into my analysis. But in my view this sense of representation is indeed an effect of ideological domination, to the extent that the 'representativity' of the rulers is actually contested by other ideologies. For the assertion of one criterion of representativity over others is a kind of domination *per se*, although it does not imply that the defeated criteria are in any sense necessarily more 'true'. Moreover, even if the principle of representation is uncontested, we can identify a disjuncture between representatives and represented simply by analysing how the rulers' policies actually affect the positions of the ruled. This procedure, as I have shown in *What Does the Ruling Class Do When It Rules?*, does not entail any recourse to hidden normative notions of 'objective interest'. The representativity of the rulers may be based on a perception of likeness or *belonging*, such that the rulers and the ruled are seen as belonging to the same universe, however defined. But it may also be based on its opposite, if the rulers are seen as possessing extraordinary qualities of understanding and as really defending the needs of the ruled. This is *charismatic* representation, by anyone from 'the man with a mission' to the flashy TV personality.

Deference is also an effect of enunciations of what is good about the present rulers. The latter are conceived as being a caste apart, possessing superior qualities, qualities which are necessary qualifications for ruling, and which the present rulers alone possess. These qualities are usually seen as deriving from descent and breeding, and deference has a clear pre-capitalist tinge. It is probably stronger in Britain than in any other advanced capitalist country, with the possible exception of Japan. It is often sustained in personalistic and lineal clientelistic networks, in which petty favours are exchanged for subservience.

A common mistake is to assume that force can rule alone, whereas the truth is that force can *never* rule alone. This is so because, religious mythologies to the contrary, one can only rule over the living. And even when disobedience leads to certain death, one can always choose either resistance and death or obedience and life. *Fear* is the effect of ideological domination that brings about acceptance of the second solution. My intention here is not to preach some heroic morality, but simply to advance our understanding of the history of rule, obedience and resistance. The fact is that men and women have, in certain situations, chosen certain death instead of life and obedience. It is therefore important to emphasize that force and violence operate as a form of rule only through the ideological mechanism of fear. The reverse is not true, however: fear does not become operative only when backed by force and violence — the clearest case in point being the religious fear of supernatural punishment.

Death is not the only sanction for disobedience. There is also the fear of being excommunicated or of losing one's job. There is the fear of right-wing (foreign or domestic) retaliation, and of a ruthless left-wing exercise of power.

Fear means that beyond the frontiers of obedience there is, *in the current situation*, only nothingness, the non-existence of chaos, darkness, suffering and death. Fear plays a great role in the maintenance of bourgeois-democratic rule.

Resignation, like fear, derives from considerations of what is possible in the given situation. But whereas obedience out of fear is contingent upon the presently prevailing constellations of force and is quite compatible with maintaining a belief in the possibility of a better alternative in the future, resignation has more deep-seated connotations. It connotes a more profoundly pessimistic view of the possibilities of change. In this context the term is used for designating a form of obedience that derives from conceptions of the practical impossibility of a better alternative, rather than of the repressive strength of the powers in existence. This resignation may stem from received and accepted statements that all power corrupts, also alternative power, that the forces for a change are too few, divided, incompetent, or unreliable, that an alternative society would be unable to maintain itself, democratically, economically or militarily. The majority of the vast numbers of ex-Socialists and ex-Communists exemplify the workings of resignation.

The force-and-consent dichotomy is grossly inadequate for the analysis and understanding of domination. It tells us nothing about the very different kinds of non-coercive acquiescence and obedience. It neglects the necessary ideological mediation of 'force' or sanctions, and fails to see that consent is largely governed by the constellation of force in a given situation.[37] Implicit in the dichotomy seems to be, in most cases, the totally mistaken notion that domination is ensured either by ideology (consensus, including 'false consciousness') or by non-ideology.

The Weberian problematic of legitimacy deals only with interpellations of what is good or right, which we have shown to be but one mode of ideological interpellation among others. Of the three kinds of legitimation analysed by Weber, his 'traditional' form of legitimate domination roughly corresponds to the above concept of deference. ('Charismatic domination' is a special case of the operation of a sense of representation.) Weber's peculiar emphasis on 'legal-rational' domination stems from his highly charact-eristic concern with how domination is organized rather than with how it is ensured. It refers to the norms for obedience by the 'staff' of a given regime, in this case the 'bureacracy', which obeys orders issued in due legal form by the proper authorities. What Weber had in mind Marxists would call the bourgeois state — that state based upon the principle of representative government established by the bourgeois revolutions. Underlying Weber's legal-rational form of legitimate domination, then, is the sense of representation. Indeed, Weber may be said to have imposed upon himself the rather arbitrary restriction of not dealing with illegitimate forms of rule.

Our schema of ideological domination may also be seen as a specification of the Gramscian concept of hegemony, which in Gramsci's own work tended to be confined within the force-and-consent dichotomy. Any existing hegemony would thus involve, in varying combinations, the sense of representation, accommodation, deference, and resigna-tion. A strategy for hegemony would primarily involve linking the interpellated revolutionary class to the strategic organization through a sense of representation. But with regard to other subaltern classes, this might include a kind of deference to the central revolutionary class, as well as accommodation with allied classes and, perhaps, their resignation at the possibility of other solutions. To the extent that the strategy aims at neutralizing sectors of the ruling class otherwise than by force and fear, it would concentrate on bringing about resignation (with regard to the practical possibility of maintaining the present order) and a sense of inevitability, while holding out the possibility of accommodation.

The proposed typology clearly reveals the limitations of the current concern that the populations of advanced capitalist countries have a decreasing sense of being represented. Contrary to the fears of the 'neo-conservatives' in the Trilateral Commission and right-wing US journals, and contrary to the hopes of various radicals, this trend does not necessarily entail a weakening of the existing regimes. It could be more or less compensated, and even overcompensated to the point of strengthening these regimes, by other, increasingly important mechanisms of subjection, such as accommodation, fear and resignation.

2. Legitimacy, Consensus, Class Consciousness: Archaisms and Problems in Political Theory

Political theory has long treated the role of ideology in the maintenance and change of political power primarily in terms of the three categories: legitimacy, consensus, and revolutionary class consciousness, together with their related sets of questions and concerns. (Throughout this essay I have taken a critical distance from that variant of political theory which is largely synonomous with the history of ideas.)

Legitimacy refers to a quality of government, whether or not the latter is based upon the prevailing criteria of 'the right to rule'. A government either does or does not *have* legitimacy; it *is* or *is not* legitimate. Consensus, or consent, on the other hand, refers to 'civil society', and in this context to its relations with the government. Civil society does or does not consent to a given regime. According to liberal and democratic conceptions of government, legitimacy should derive from, and be grounded upon, a societal consensus. By contrast, the problematic of class consciousness focuses on class division instead of the consensual unity of society, and its main concern is with political change. Revolutionary class consciousness of the dominated class or classes is regarded as an essential, though not necessarily sufficient, precondition of fundamental political change.

These notions have constituted the foci of a voluminous discussion about bases, problems, and crises of legitimacy;[38] the content and range of consensus;[39] the preconditions and the existence or not of revolutionary class consciousness.[40] I shall not delve into the specific merits and mistakes of any individual contributions, although it should be noted that some perceptive criticisms and comments have been made within these various problematics. My concern is rather with the sets of assumptions and questions that constitute these approaches, with the problematics of reflection and research governed by the notions of legitimacy, consensus, and class consciousness. Basing myself on the preceding sections of this essay, I shall argue three points in connection with these problematics. First, they are essentially flawed as approaches to empirical analysis, and their questions concerning power and ideology should be radically reformulated. Second, the reason for their analytical inadequacy is that they are rooted in a normative philosophy deriving from the bourgeois revolution. Third, however, they all refer obliquely to important problems, which can be fruitfully broached once we insert the three notions into a problematic different from that of the philosophy of the bourgeois revolution.

There are at least four characteristics common to the problematics of legitimacy, consensus, and class consciousness that severely limit their usefulness as foci of empirical analysis and guides to conscious political practice.

1. They all have a subjectivist conception of history,

according to which political processes are decided by unitary conscious subjects, legitimate or illegitimate governments, consenting or dissenting peoples, consciously revolutionary or unconscious classes. They leave no room for de-centred constraints and fissures, contradictions and reinforcements, such as are inscribed in the economic and political structure and process. Nor do they allow for the complexities of social heterogeneity and compartmentalization; for processes with unintended consequences and diverse, often unnoticed temporalities;[41] and for the ever-ongoing formation and re-formation of subjective identifies.

2. They are all idealist in the sense that they view legitimacy, consensus, and class consciousness as ideological configurations separated and separable from material matrices of practices, organizational forms, and relations of force.

3. They all basically assume a simplistic, rationalist motivation of human beings. The members of a society are assumed to relate to a given regime in a conscious, homogeneous (at least among large sub-groups), and consistent manner. *Either* a regime has legitimacy *or* it does not; people obey *either* because of normative consent *or* because of physical coercion; *either* the dominated class or classes have a conception of revolutionary change, *or* they accept the status quo or are content with piecemeal reforms; people act *either* on the basis of true knowledge *or* on the basis of false ideas. Thus, no systematic attention is paid to the interdependence of force and consent, to the existence and interrelation of different kinds of knowledge, to the wide range of competing human concerns and desires, or to the possibility of discontinuous, situated motivation.

4. They usually conceive of ideology — in its relation to legitimacy, consensus, and class consciousness — as a

possession or non-possession. This approach involves the reification of ideology and systematic neglect of the way ideologies operate, constantly being communicated, competing, clashing, affecting, drowning, and silencing one another in social processes of communication. It is as such that they are, consciously and unconsciously, received, interpreted, accepted, rejected, maintained, or transformed by individuals, groups, and classes.

Moreover, the problematics of legitimacy and consensus operate with a reductionist view of ideology and ideological dynamics, in the sense that they concentrate exclusively on normative ideologies of what is good and bad. The class-consciousness problematic, on the other hand, is more complex, though in a revolutionary perspective the ideological process is usually subsumed under its cognitive dimension — true versus false knowledge. (It should be noted that all these criticisms also apply to subjectivist and idealist usages of the Gramscian concept of hegemony, currently employed in analysing existing organizations of power and conceiving strategies for social transformation.) The case against this sort of analysis has already been suggested in every preceding section; it will be discussed in more detail below. If my objections are correct, however, it may be asked why these conceptualizations figure so prominently and disastrously in contemporary political theory. The explanation has three aspects. Authors working within the three problematics mentioned above have fallen into the trap of analysing contemporary politics with the aid of notions derived from another age and another theoretical universe. This trap is then reproduced not simply because the alternative traditions to empirical analysis still have a lingering effect, but also because the criticized notions do refer to important problems for which a more adequate theory has not been available. The foundations of such a theory have been laid by Althusser's contribution. It involves a conception of history as a de-centred dialectical process without a subject and a materialist theory of ideology emancipated from all utilitarian debris; and it incorporates a number of insights from psychoanalysis and theories of discourse and communication, and is now being developed along various lines of investigation.

The lack of analytical rigour in the problematics of legitimacy, consensus, and class consciousness derives from the fact that they were not at all developed as tools of empirical analysis. Each has its roots in the *normative* problems of the bourgeois revolution; each belongs to the world of normative political philosophy. These problematics originated in the classical age of bourgeois-revolutionary struggles against dynastic and for popular-consensual legitimacy. The problematic within which class consciousness is conceived as the bearer of a new social order and as a key to social change also originated in this age, and more particularly in Hegel's philosophy of history. Thus, in the left-historicism of Lukács and Mannheim, Hegel's notion of successive *Volksgeister* bearing the World Spirit was replaced by a conception in which the consciousnesses of various classes bear the historical forms of social order.

The three problematics in question formed part either of a manifestly speculative philosophy of history (the transmutations of Hegel) or of a normative political philosophy centred on how political power *ought* to be grounded ('power ought to be legitimate'; 'it ought to be based on consent'; 'political change ought to be based on revolutionary class consciousness'; 'history ought to be made by a unitary, self-conscious subject'). They did not develop through investigation of how political regimes actually manage to stay in power, how socio-political change actually occurs. I am not saying that the ought-questions are not noble concerns, only that they do not help much in explaining what actually happens and is likely to happen. Hegemony, too, often has a normative connotation; and Gramsci himself strongly suggested that class rule *ought* to be grounded on hegemony, that ascendant classes *ought* to struggle for hegemony.

There is, of course, another important political philosophy which, in the tradition of Machiavelli, has exhibited considerably greater analytical subtlety. Machiavelli not only inspired cynical elitists of the right, but also influenced the sharp revolutionary mind of Antonio Gramsci. Of significance to Machiavelli's extraordinary perspicacity, however, was probably that he lived before the bourgeois era of popular legitimacy. His major works were thus written in a pre-bourgeois format, as an address to the prince.

Now, if all the notions described above are freed from their original philosophical sweep and inserted into a materialist and analytical problematic of power and ideology, then they all refer to valid and important topics of research and strategic political discourse. It should also be borne in mind that, before it became the centre of general and rather vacuous discussions about the ideological bases of political power, the concept of legitimacy was used by Max Weber in a much more precise and restrictive sense. Weber's sociology of domination was essentially a sociology from above, focusing on how domination was motivated and organized, not on how it actually operated or on the mechanisms through which the positions of dominator and dominated were reproduced.[42] It might be concluded that Weber saw legitimating ideology as communicated rather than possessed, and, above all, that he was concerned with the organizational contexts of legitimacy.

From a non-normative point of view, the critical issues of legitimacy are not popular distrust, discontent, or withdrawal. Not even the spread of illegal practices is really important in itself. Every state in history has nearly always had its law-breakers, bandits, smugglers, thieves, offenders against morality, dissenters, tax-evaders and deserters; and every state has frequently had to face organized forms of protest and riotous crowds.

The really crucial feature is *organized counter-claims to legitimacy*, and the effects these claims have, when put to the test, upon the loyalty and efficacy of the state apparatus. A counter-claim to legitimacy differs crucially from dissent, protest, and law-breaking, insofar as a non-governing organization claims, on whatever grounds, that it is the legitimate government or has the legitimate right to form one. The organized counter-claim may be presented either by parts of the state apparatus (usually the military) or by revolutionary organizations outside the state. However, it may short-circuit these by surging forward on the crest of the *disorganization of the legitimacy* of the existing regime. The 'disorganization of legitimacy' is an affliction of the *apparatuses of rule*, unlike the traditional conception of 'loss' of legitimacy, which pertains to the *ideas* of the *ruled*. Such a disorganization occurs, as in the collapse of the Romanov, Habsburg, and Hohenzollern empires, when the repressive forces refuse to defend, or abstain from defending, the regime in the face of mounting popular protest.

In this regard, the stability of the political regimes of the advanced capitalist countries is rather impressive. Apart from the three-day Kapp-Lüttwitz putsch in Germany in 1920, the last military coup in what are now the seventeen leading OECD countries took place nearly two centuries ago: the Eighteenth Brumaire of the first Napoleon in 1799, or ten years later, when the Swedish army deposed the king (only to hand over power immediately to a Constituent Assembly of the Estates). The last full-scale civil war occurred in Finland in 1918, and the last-but-one in the

United States. Fascism came to power through constitutional channels, as did Pétain in 1940 and de Gaulle in 1958. The dismantling of democracy in Austria and Japan in the 1930s was carried out from above by the constitutional government of the time. The last revolutionary change of government in these countries was the collapse of the Hohenzollern and Habsburg monarchies in the late autumn of 1918. The last working-class insurrections took place in Germany in the 1930s, or in 1934 if we include the last-ditch attempt of the Austrian workers to preserve democracy. Ever since the Popular Front period, the Communist parties of these countries have in practice recognized elected bourgeois governments that allow as legitimate the basic rights of working-class organization and opposition. The only (self-defeating) exception is the German KPD, which in 1949-53 called for an all-out offensive against the Adenauer regime. In the final days of May 1968 the French Communist Party and the Socialist Left did call for a new government, but when de Gaulle made it clear that he was not going to withdraw, all the significant formations of the French Left immediately stepped down. In recent Eurocommunist discourse this legitimacy of elected bourgeois-democratic governments has been explicitly enunciated as a principle. Although there may be a crisis of certain liberal ideologies in contemporary advanced capitalism, these countries certainly show no sign of a 'crisis' or of serious 'problems' of legitimacy. Many of them may be experiencing a decrease in normative support and encountering increased disrespect. But this process seems to involve a shift from a sense of representation and deference to accommodation and a sense of inevitability, rather than a crisis of domination. Another matter is the fact that these regimes face an *opposition*, smaller or larger, more or less threatening, above all in France and Italy.

I do not wish to suggest, however, that legitimacy is of no

importance. It was crucial to the success of the October Revolution that the Kerensky government was not considered legitimate by the mass of soldiers and railway workers (key workers for the movement of troops in those days before full motorization); and that the Bolshevik insurrection worked through the Petrograd Soviet, then regarded as a legitimate government by broad layers of the working class and soldiery. Conversely, the main body of the German civil service considered the Kapp-Lüttwitz government as illegitimate, and the bulk of the army regarded it as only potentially legitimate (if it proved capable of holding out). These features sealed the fate of the putsch in the face of a general strike. In France the fact that the army confirmed the legitimacy of the Fifth Republic decided the outcome of May 1968.

Clearly, the contemporary advanced capitalist countries have not become immune to crises of governmental legitimacy. Indeed, such crises are likely to follow major Communist and left-socialist advances in France and Italy, just to mention the most immediate probabilities, and a foreboding of this was discernible in the American and West German threats against Communist participation in the Italian government. Nevertheless, diffuse and unorganized disaffection, scepticism, and cynicism do not amount to a 'crisis of legitimacy'.

From a normative point of view, there is a clear, all-important dividing line between force and consent. In practice, however, the two are interrelated in a complex manner. The course of action to which one consents is always dependent on the situation, on what is perceived as existing and possible — in other words, on a constellation of forces. Any regime can produce its own social consent by presenting all outright opposition with impossible odds. Such consent may not involve a widespread sense of representation among the ruled, but it need not be based on massive fear. It could instead be rooted in resignation, deference, and accommodation — which, in many or most bourgeois-democratic countries, are probably more important components of consensus than is a sense of representation.

So far we have made no explicit distinction between 'consensus' and 'consent', but at this point it is necessary to differentiate between the two. To say that any regime can produce its own consent is not exactly to say that it can produce its own consensus. Whereas 'consent' connotes 'agreement to' something or somebody, 'consensus' refers primarily to 'agreement among' a group of people. The key analytical aspects of consensus and consent are not, as normative theory would have it, located in society, among the ruled. The really critical factor is a basic *consensus among the ruling groups themselves, and consent to their legitimacy by members of the state apparatus*, particularly the repressive apparatus. Dictatorships may be more or less unpopular. Yet they fall not through lack of popular consent, but through a shift in the relations of force, in which popular discontent is an intermediary rather than independent causal variable. Often the relations of force have changed because disastrous external wars have, in varying degree, broken up the repressive forces and caused dissension among the ruling groups in the face of reactivated popular protest. The relations of force also change when the ruling groups fall out among themselves — often when a dictator has died and the regime is refused legitimacy by sections of the repressive forces. It is usually during such a process of disintegration that popular forces break onto the arena and may play a decisive historical role.

If it is true that the line of demarcation between force and consent is intrinsically blurred, then another normative measure is needed — unless, that is, we are to fall into brute cynicism à la Samuel Huntington, or into a pessimistic anarchism of the kind that Adorno and Horkheimer expressed in their *Dialectic of Enlightenment* and that resounds in Foucault's later work. In my opinion, such a normative evaluation should apply directly to the institutions of a regime, rather than to the way they are maintained. It should apply, that is, to the rights and powers these institutions grant, in practice, to different groups and classes in society, as well as to the nature and amount of the sanctions they mete out, whether or not they are 'popular'. That is, we should look at the existence and practical degree of freedom of speech, publication, association, assembly, candidacy, and voting, the manner of counting votes, the accessibility of means of popular initiative, control and self-management.

The widespread view of revolutionary class consciousness as a key to social change now appears rather peculiar in light of the historical record. So far, at least, no great modern social revolution, bourgeois or socialist, has ever been made by a unified class subject demanding a completely new social order. Rather, such revolutions have been effected in particular conjunctures when the relations of force have changed in such a way as to undermine the old regime — in other words, through the emergence of economic, political, and ideological contradictions and situations of uneven development, both within the society and in its external relations, disarticulating the previous totality and its system of affirmations and sanctions. They have been consciously made when various forces, with different immediate demands pertaining to the conjuncture, have come together. The social-revolutionary import of these demands — bread, peace, land, independence, popular representative government, an end to repression — has stemmed from a constellation of clashing class forces and their organized expressions, through which certain historical social alternatives are ruled out and others opened up.[43] That is, the dynamic of revolutions hitherto has not been one of a revolutionary class ideology envisaging and demanding a total transformation of the existing society and putting this ideology into practice. Rather, the process has gained momentum in a situation when the sustaining matrix of the regime in existence is crumbling through specific, limited and *per se* often quite 'reformist' demands, often arising out of the new acute crisis situation itself. The character of the situation gave these demands revolutionary implications, and a revolutionary ideology developed and spread among the masses in a collective process involving the most varied struggles and experiences. It seems that the most important dimensions of ideological change in this process are those concerning what exists and what is possible. Old forms of oppression come to the forefront and new ones are immediately noticed, and the range of perceived possibilities widens. While the prospect of revolutions impelled by prior revolutionary class consciousness cannot be categorically excluded, it seems much more likely that future social revolutions will take forms rather similar to those of the past. Attempts to uncover and quantify revolutionary class consciousness in a particular situation seem, therefore, to be of rather limited interest and importance. The possibilities for revolutionary change should be derived from the likelihood of economic and political crisis, and from the existence of materially organized alternatives, rather than from the state of mind of a class.

Despite all this, it does not follow that class consciousness is unimportant. A particular class-identity and class-purpose is crucial to the development of class organizations, which are the pivotal agents of social change. And, other things being equal, the more this class consciousness is spread and practised in action among the members of a dominated class, and the clearer and more advanced is its view of an alternative future, the more likely a social transformation is to succeed and prosper — *if and when* a revolutionary situation, or a less condensed period of possible transition from one society to another, actually opens up. A pre-existent *organized* revolutionary ideology — that is, an organization of some size with a revolutionary perspective — is of course also a very important variable in a situation of acute crisis. This was shown *a contrario* in the failure of even a thorough-going democratic revolution in Germany in 1918, due to the complete absence of *any* revolutionary perspective in the leading organs of Social Democracy. Generally speaking, the more qualified the ruled at the point where their subjection can no longer be sustained, the more they can achieve.

VI
Social Change and the Power of Ideology

The emphasis of the two last chapters lay on the role of ideology in the organization and the maintenance of power. Thereby we pointed to and stressed the complex, shifting and conflict-rent character of this role, far from the grey, solid monotony suggested by the common metaphor of ideology as social 'cement'. Against idealist and subjectivist conceptions of political crisis and political change, the materially situated character of ideologies and subjectivities and the crucial role of organizational structures and material supports were stressed. On this basis, however, we should look into a few aspects of ideological dynamics proper, into the operation of the power of ideology in processes of social change.

1. Processes of Ideological Mobilization

In this section we shall only touch upon that form of social change with which Marxists have generally been most concerned: namely, compressed processes of change involving masses of people and aiming at a transformation of the social and political regime. The classical bourgeois and socialist revolutions are examples of this kind, but so too are the recent revolutions in Iran and Nicaragua; various revolts that did not develop into revolutions, such as the French May; and, on the other hand, the fascist conquests of power and counter-revolutionary mobilizations.

Instead of confirming the simple theoretical counter-position, according to which a regime falls when the sense of its illegitimacy has spread sufficiently among the ruled population, or when dissent or revolutionary class consciousness has grown too great, history usually presents us with a much more complex picture. A situation of acute crisis emerges when, for whatever reason, the matrix of affirmations and sanctions underpinning the given regime and the ruling ideology breaks up. And if the regime is faced with organized counter-claims to legitimacy, or a profound disorganization of its legitimacy in the eyes of significant sections of the state apparatus, or dissent within itself, or any combination of these, then the regime faces a revolutionary situation. So much has already been said above. What we must now examine is the role and functioning of ideology in drawing masses of people into these situations of crisis, revolution, and counter-revolution. Instead of looking for the Subject of revolutionary (or counter-revolutionary) class consciousness, we must try to understand the actual processes of ideological mobilization.

Ideological mobilization may be said to involve setting a common agenda for a mass of people — that is to say, summing up the dominant aspect or aspects of the crisis, identifying the crucial target, the essence of evil, and defining what is possible and how it should be achieved. Such mobilization develops through a breach in the regime's matrix of affirmations and sanctions, which in normal times ensures compromise or acquiescence and the successful sanctioning of oppositional forces. This breach grows to the extent that it is itself successfully affirmed in the practice of demonstrations, acts of insubordination and revolt, and so on. A successful ideological mobilization is always translated into or manifested in practices of political mobilization.

Ideological mobilizations, even of an explicitly class character, always have a strong existential component and are never reducible to revolutionary class consciousness. An intense ideological commitment involves a transformation and mobilization of the individual subjectivity of those committed, a subordination of their own suffering and possible death to a meaning-of-life defined by the ideology. Indeed, in a revolutionary mobilization the meaning of life is itself set by the revolutionary agenda. Political-ideological mobilizations are not fixed in class and 'popular-democratic' interpellations alone. Their success hinges largely upon their capacity to tap and harness the existential dimensions of human subjectivity. In the classical age of the labour movement this was often done through incorporation of the transmuted fervour and puritanism of Christian and Jewish religion. Today, however, the problem is to relate to the secularized, post-Puritan age of 'self-valorization' (as it is termed on the extreme Left in Italy) in the advanced capitalist countries.

Ideological mobilization implies the fusion and condensation of several ideological discourses into a single major threat, usually expressed in a simple slogan. Thus, in all revolutions that have changed the class character of the state, elements of class ideologies have been fused with other types of ideological mobilization, religious or national, for example; and the revolutionary mobilization has always taken a conjunctural ideological form ('Peace!', 'Down with Batista!' or the Shah or Somoza). The class character of revolutions is not necessarily expressed in the main slogans of ideological mobilization. Indeed, in the successful revolutions of the past, these have usually *not* been class interpellations, but have been determined by the constellation of class forces actually mobilized.

In the ideological mobilization for the Russian October Revolution, direct class interpellations were certainly very important. The Bolsheviks mobilized with tremendous success using such slogans as 'All power to the Soviets!' and 'Land to the peasants!'. But it is noteworthy that on the eve of insurrection the mobilization took forms predominantly much more specific than those of 'class against class'.[44] Contrary to what a simplistic conception might lead us to expect, revolutionary polarizations in, say, the French and Russian revolutions — to take the most common paradigms — did not directly pit the ideologies of the two main classes against each other as positional ideologies on a single battlefield. Rather, the class ideologies confronted each other as inclusive/exclusive ideologies. Each class tended to constitute a historically-inclusive universe of its own, including several classes and strata and non-class subjectivities set against an alien force excluded from the former multi-class/non-class universe as 'usurpers', 'foreign agents', or counter-revolutionaries (working, that is, against the earlier, broader revolutions of 1789 and February 1917).

Paradoxically, it is this non-class definition of the principal contradiction that has paved the way for the physical and/or social destruction of the defeated class or class-fraction through a vigorous revolution from below; whereas a class-positional definition has usually been connected either with administered revolutions from above or with a reformist deal. This paradox becomes understandable if we remember that class is a position within a wider world that also includes the opposite class. However, the inverse is not true — that non-class definitions of the principal contradiction usually are revolutionary. They are more often part of class-collaborationist ideologies and stances, singling out foreign machinations or particularly 'selfish' or 'parasitic' groups as the main enemy.

Significant ideological mobilizations do not, of course,

spring from the ruins of the material matrix of a previously dominant ideology. Nor do they seem to owe much to the correctness or conjunctural adequacy of elaborate pro-grammes or grand theories. The key figures in processes of ideological mobilization are not theoreticians and writers of books, but orators, preachers, journalists, pamphleteers, politicians, and initiators of bold practical action. At this point, however, an important distinction must be made between, on the one hand, ideological mass mobilization for political change and, on the other, the problems of successfully defending and consolidating a victorious revolution. In the process of breaking up a regime in crisis, the weight of immediate action and single-minded devotion is paramount. But after a revolution, the degree of articulation, autonomy, and strength of class ideology, class organization, and related theories and programmes crucially determines the fate of the exploited classes that have been mobilized — for these are their only assets in the face of the new state during the construction of a new society.

Despite the immense variety of the concrete historical forms of ideological mobilization, it seems possible to locate some of their principal motive forces. But first we must make clear that the only kind of mobilization with which we are directly concerned is large-scale, rapid ideological mobilization of significance in threatening or reorienting a regime. Further, we are here focusing on mobilizations that take place in a situation where the material matrix of the previously dominant ideology crumbles away, and not where, for example, a new mode of production is emerging and new classes are being formed, together with a new basic matrix. (We have already touched on the latter case above.) What then is the basis for a massive new ideological subjection-qualification against the present ideological system? A new ideological mobilization involves two processes: the decomposition of an old system of qualification-subjection, and the recomposition of a new one. We have already dealt with the first aspect, referring to the emergence of a contradiction between qualification and subjection, and to processes of uneven development that disarticulate the dominant ideology from its sustaining totality of affirmations and sanctions.

The processes through which the matrix of sanctions-affirmations has broken up and ushered in a major socio-political crisis have generally been of two main kinds. One has been defeat, or imminent danger of defeat, in external war, crucial in both the Russian (1905 and 1917) and Chinese revolutions. For during wartime the population is already mobilized by the regime in power; while defeat is perhaps the most blatant and painful disaffirmation of a system of domination, one that seriously weakens its powers of internal sanctioning and its repressive apparatus. The second kind of massive break-up has occurred when a regime becomes isolated from sections of its own class base — as Batista was in the late 1950s, as the Shah became in relation to the Tehran bazaar, as the Somoza clan became when a new bourgeoisie developed out of the boom of the 1960s and 1970s, and as the pre-fascist bourgeois regimes became in Italy and Germany. Successful wars of independence seem always to have involved a major element of support or more or less benevolent neutrality from classes not exploited in the Marxist sense, even when these movements have been led by Marxists and Communists. This was the case in Vietnam, where the Viet Minh and NLF had a broad social base. The Pathet Lao was led by a member of the royal family, and the Khmer Rouge grew into a major force after the Americans and the far Right had deposed Sihanouk. The Algerian FLN had a non-Communist leadership and strong support from sectors of the bourgeoisie and capitalist notables. Counter-revolutionary mobilizations, of course, involve the major sections of the former ruling class itself; but they become dangerous to a revolution controlling the state apparatus only (short of foreign intervention) if they can arouse large sectors of the popular classes by or for which the revolution was made. As all these cases testify, therefore, an established system of power and exploitation has such enormous strength that it can very rarely be challenged by the exploited or ruled classes on their own.

We now have to ask what governs the recomposition of a new ideological system. One way of framing an answer to this is to start from the bases on which an ideological mobilization against the present may take place. There are three logical possibilities that seem to have provided the three major sources in known history, although in a total process of mobilization these are not mutually exclusive in practice.

First, it is possible to mobilize on the basis of the *past*, of what has existed, of past experiences, values, symbols, and so on. This is done by reactionaries and counter-revolutionaries, but it is also often an important component of nationalist mobilization. Revolutionaries may also revive past experiences of organization, struggle, and ideological formation rendered latent or forgotten by defeats or repression and by the victories or boom-periods enjoyed by the enemy. In this way the October Revolution fed on the experiences of 1905, after the patriotic euphoria had been dissipated by massacres at the front and food shortages at the rear; and, similarly, the radicals of the late 1960s would resurrect the revolutionary traditions of the labour movement. Sometimes, as in Iran, the basis of mobilization has a fundamentally ambiguous character, involving both reactionary and revolutionary elements. Now, if such *mobilization by revival* is to be successful, it must be possible for the experiences and values of the past to enter into the order of the day. Thus when the crisis in Russia opened up in early 1917, under the impact of disastrous military defeats and the breakdown of transportation and food supply, the experiences of 1905 — when the same regime had suffered the collapse of its authority, with its military might humiliated and tied up in the Far East — became directly relevant. Fascism offered both a diagnosis of and a therapy for the socio-political crisis of the 1930s by relating it to the First World War experiences of national unity, violence, final defeat, dislocation, and frustration. In the very different radicalization of the late 1960s, the US war in Vietnam and the upsurge of strikes and demonstrations gave new credibility, in many people's eyes, to classical Marxist conceptions of imperialism and the class struggle. And it was no accident that this new movement went furthest in France and Italy, where these old working-class traditions were strongest, while petering out most rapidly in the United States, where they were at their weakest.

A second major kind of ideological mobilization takes place on the basis of another present reality. We might call this *mobilization by example*. Thus the French revolutions of 1789, 1830, and 1848 triggered similar attempts in most of Western and Central Europe; the October Revolution sent shock-waves over almost all the globe; and the Chinese and Cuban revolutions inspired attempts at imitation in other countries of Asia and Latin America, respectively. This is a very potent source of mobilization, most clearly expressed, perhaps, in the existence of more than eighty Communist parties throughout the world. These were founded under the impetus of a revolution that occurred more than sixty years ago, and whose potency derives from a change in prevailing conceptions of what is possible. However, mobilizations by example have usually failed in their immediate thrust. A successful example may discredit rival forms of opposition, but it can rarely be repeated: both because the constellation of forces is hardly ever the same in other societies, and because the victorious revolution is also an educative experience for the ruling classes of other countries. This second kind of mobilization includes the inspiration of counter-examples. The striking-power of fascism, for example, can hardly be grasped unless we keep in mind that the revolutionary labour movement was not only its main enemy but also a model of organization and ideological inculcation.

Finally, it is possible to mobilize the future against the present: for example, as a goal for a just society, as a guarantee of ultimate victory in present struggles or of salvation from present suffering, or as an imminent mythological paradise. In the really dramatic socio-political mobilizations, however, the future has predominantly taken the form of an imminent threat flowing from current tendencies, which has called for pre-emptive action in the present. We might term this process *mobilization by anticipatory fear*, to distinguish it from fear as a mechanism of maintaining domination. The French Revolution was driven forward by this kind of mobilization — from the peasants' Great Fear of an aristocratic conspiracy in 1789, to that fear of a royal conspiracy with foreign enemies that brought the Jacobins to power. Similarly, fear of a counter-revolution that had already assumed material shape in Kornilov was a crucial aspect of the Russian workers' turn to the Bolsheviks in the autumn of 1917. Indeed, the Bolshevik October insurrection began as a series of measures explicitly intended to secure the already-existing revolution against a counter-revolutionary move by Kerensky — a fact that was very important in the achievement of broad unity within the Petrograd Soviet.

2. Political Subjects and Ideological Drift

The ideological system of societies in expanded or declining reproduction is never static but in constant flux, with changing practices and conditions. Of all these kinds of ideological change, large and small, one should be mentioned here, because it has a special pertinence to the character of a regime. It is not a dramatic mobilization that poses an acutely serious, sometimes deadly, threat to the powers in existence, but involves a change *in* rather than *of* the dominant discourse.

This ideological change derives from a change in the universe of political subjects, other than the displacement of the rulers. The most obvious case is, of course, the maturation of new generations, who in a changing society have been subjected-qualified under conditions different from the old. This poses particular problems to regimes strongly shaped by dramatic conjunctures of the past, counter-revolutionary as well as revolutionary regimes.

But new political subjects, who speak for themselves, may also emerge through political and social struggles. The universe of political subjects may be widened, either through the extension of legal rights, such as the franchise, or through a process of ideological and political autonomization. An important ideological shift of this kind took place in Sweden in the 1930s, when the peasantry reconquered its autonomy from the bourgeois bloc and allied itself, with a voice of its own, with Social Democracy. In the last decade there has been a significant process of ideological autonomization of women in the advanced capitalist world.

However, the range of political subjects who are allowed to speak or who are listened to may also be narrowed. Bourgeois ideologists to the contrary, history is no teleological process of widening citizenship. The disenfranchisement of Southern blacks after Reconstruction in the United States and the ghetto-confinement of all left-wing movements during the Cold War, as well as the banning of all opposition by all kinds of dictatorship, exemplify the frequent occurrence of a narrowing of political 'citizenship'.

Now, the point here is not simply the self-evident fact that the ensemble of ideological utterances changes with variations of the number and character of participants in ideological discussion. It is rather that the discourse of the rulers still in place is affected, undergoing an ideological drift. The conquest of universal suffrage did not displace the bourgeoisie, but it meant that bourgeois discourse changed, having to adapt to the political rights of the working class. Similarly, the realignment of the Swedish peasantry in the 1930s left capitalism intact but meant a permutation of the dominant ideological system, whereby capital accumulation remained an important theme, but where other components of bourgeois ideology, such as individualism and inegalitarian incentives, were subdued by themes of collective solidarity and equality. Inversely, the restriction of opposition not only silences those excommunicated. It also narrows the ideological range of those still allowed to speak. Over time these processes may bring about quite considerable ideological drift in the dominant discourse and significantly affect the practices of those in power.

The power of ideology operates not only in conjunctures of high drama, but in slow, gradual processes as well. Ideologies not only cement systems of power; they may also cause them to crumble and set them drifting like sandbanks, still there though not in the same place and shape. Yet both cases will involve complex concatenations of forces and voices, in which patterns and relationships may be distinguished and rendered amenable to materialist explanation. It is to this theoretically and politically central task of explanation that this essay set out to contribute. The essay must end now, but the task has only just begun.

Notes

1. *What Does the Ruling Class Do When It Rules?*, London 1978.
2. See my *Science, Class and Society*, London 1976, pp. 66ff.
3. A key theoretical statement is Marx's Preface to his *Contribution to the Critique of Political Economy*; another is the passage from *The Eighteenth Brumaire*, cited in n.5 below. Of the letters by Marx and Engels dealing with the ideological struggle for and of a proletarian party, see, for example, their circular letter to Bebel, Liebknecht and others of September 1879, Marx and Engels, *Selected Correspondence*, Moscow 1965, pp. 321-7, esp. pp. 326-7.
4. Engels to Mehring, July 14, 1893, *Selected Correspondence*, p. 459.
5. Cf. the overview by Carol Johnson, 'The Problem of Reformism and Marx's Theory of Fetishism', *New Left Review*, 119 (January-February, 1980). In *The Eighteenth Brumaire* Marx made an important general theoretical statement about ideology and applied it to the rival monarchist factions of the bourgeoisie: 'A whole superstructure of different and specifically formed feelings, illusions, modes of thought and views of life arises on the basis of the different forms of property, of the social conditions of existence. The whole class creates and forms these out of its material foundations and the corresponding social relations. The single individual, who derives these feelings, etc. through tradition and upbringing, may well imagine that they form the real determinants and the starting-point of his activity. The Orleanist and Legitimist fractions each tried to make out to their opponents and themselves that they were divided by their adherence to the

two royal houses; facts later proved that it was rather the division between their interests which forbade the unification of the royal houses. A distinction is made in private life between what a man thinks and says of himself and what he really is and does. In historical struggles one must make a still sharper distinction between the phrases and fantasies of the parties and their real organization and real interests, between their conception of themselves and what they really are. Orleanists and Legitimists found themselves side by side in the republic making equal claims. Each side wanted to secure the *restoration* of its *own* royal house against the other; this had no other meaning than that each of the *two great interests* into which the bourgeoisie is divided — landed property and capital — was endeavouring to restore its own supremacy and the subordination of the other interest.' Karl Marx, *Surveys from Exile*, London 1977.

Marx's main conclusion here may, of course, be maintained without the epistemological problematic of 'interests' and 'illusions', showing the historical linking of the rival royal houses with different class fractions.

6. In the Preface to *A Contribution to the Critique of Political Economy* Marx stated that 'mankind always sets itself only such tasks as it can solve; since looking at the matter more closely, it will always be found that the task itself arises only when the material conditions for its solution already exist or are at least in the process of formation'.

7. See the very interesting overview, J. Clarke, C. Critcher, R. Johnson, eds., *Working Class Culture*, London 1979.

8. F. Châtelet, ed., *Histoire des idéologies*, 3 vols., Paris 1978; vol. 1, pp. 10-11. In fact, this massive work is a rather traditional, quasi-encyclopedic history of ideas.

9. The quotation is from Williams, *Marxism and Literature*, Oxford 1977, pp. 81-2. Cf. Anthony Barnett, 'Raymond Williams and Marxism: A Rejoinder to Terry Eagleton', *New Left Review*, 99 (1976).

10. R. Johnson, 'Three Problematics: Elements of a Theory of Working-Class Culture', in *Working Class Culture*, p. 234. (Emphasis omitted.) In a very valuable contribution, neither sectarian nor uncritically ecumenical, Johnson here discusses

classical Marxism, the Hoggart-Thompson-Williams concern with working-class culture, and Althusserian 'structuralism'.

11. L. Althusser, 'Ideology and Ideological State Apparatuses', in *Lenin and Philosophy*, London, NLB, 1971, p. 164. Johnson may have confused the Althusserian theory of the social operation of ideology with an exploration of the psychodynamic processes forming human subjectivity which is inspired by Lacan's interpretation of psychoanalysis, and is perfectly legitimate as far as it goes.

12. See Nicos Poulantzas's critique of Foucault in his *State, Power, Socialism*, London, NLB, 1978 — a work which, in its style and preoccupations, is at the same time obviously inspired by Foucault's writings.

13. Among the more important contributions are; in alphabetical order: A. Badiou, P. Balmès, *De l'idéologie*, (Paris 1976); Center For Contemporary Cultural Studies, *On Ideology*, London 1978; R. Coward, J. Ellis, *Language and Materialism*, London 1977; E. de Ipola, 'Critica a la teoria de Althusser sobre la ideologia', *Cuadernos de CISCO* No. 4, n.d.; P. Hirst, *On Law and Ideology*, London 1979; R. Johnson, *op. cit.*; G. Labica, 'De l'Egalité. Propositions pour une enquête sur les ideologies dans le mode de production capitaliste', *Dialectiques* Nos. 1-2, 6 (1974); E. Laclau, *Politics and Ideology*, London, NLB, 1977; C. Mouffe, 'State ideology and power', (paper presented at ECPR/CPSA workshop in Brussels in 1979); M. Pécheux, *Les vérités de la palice*, Paris 1975; J. Rancière, *La leçon d'Althusser*, Paris 1974. Simultaneously there has been a spurt of other general works on ideology, particularly in France. See P. Ansart, *Les idéologies politiques*, Paris 1974; idem, *Idéologies, conflits, pouvoirs*, Paris 1977; J. Baudrillard, *Pour une critique de l'économie politique du signe*, París 1972; F. Dumont, *Les idéologies*, Paris 1974; A. Gouldner, *The Dialectic of Ideology and Technology*, New York 1978; J. Larrain, *The Concept of Ideology*, London 1979; E. Maffesoli, *Logique de la domination*, Paris 1976; J. C. Merquior, *The Veil and the Mask*, London 1979; C. Summer, *Reading Ideologies*, London 1979; D. Vidal, *Essai sur l'idéologie*, Paris 1971.

This literature deserves an extended evaluation, which cannot be attempted here. I will confine myself to two remarks only: the reader who wants an overview of the various treatments of ideology hitherto will find a very good introduction in the work by Larrain; the work which I personally have found most the original and interesting is Gouldner's. This work departs from Gouldner's, however, by putting the linguistic dimension of ideologies between brackets and by adopting a broader definition of ideology. Gouldner sees ideologies as 'symbol systems that serve to justify and to mobilize public projects of social reconstruction' (pp. 54-55), a definition which is too narrow for my concerns.

14. A recent example is Laclau, who writes: 'Surplus-value constitutes *simultaneously* the relation between capitalists and workers and the antagonism between them; or rather it constitutes that relation as an antagonistic one'. (*Politics and Ideology*, p. 104, emphasis in the original.)

15. The differences between the problematics of Althusser and Gramsci has been cogently argued, from a Gramscian point of view, by Mouffe, 'State, Ideology and Power'.

16. M. Foucault, *L'Ordre du discours*, Paris 1971, *La Volonté du savoir*, Paris 1976, *Discipline and Punish*, New York 1977.

17. L. Althusser, 'Ideology and Ideological State Apparatuses', pp. 168ff. Emphasis and footnote omitted.

18. Coward and Ellis give a valuable and accessible overview of several of these aspects.

19. On role theory, see B. J. Biddle and E. J. Thomas, eds., *Role Theory: Concepts and Research* (New York 1966), R. Dahrendorf, *Homo Sociologicus* (4th ed. Köln and Opladen 1964), T. Sarbin-V. Allen, 'Role Theory', in G. Lindzey and E. Aronson, eds., *Handbook of Social Psychology* (2nd ed., Reading Mass. 1968) vol. 1.

20. The Barcelona anarchist Garcia Oliver, quoted from R. Fraser, *The Blood of Spain*, New York 1979, p. 545.

21. One such attempt has been undertaken by Paul Hirst and his associates, leading in their case to an abandonment of historical materialism. (Perhaps we should add 'for the time being', given their rapidly shifting positions in the past.) See Hirst, *On Law and Ideology*, and A. Cutler, B. Hindess, P. Hirst and A. Hussain *Marx's Capital and Capitalism Today*, 2 vols., London 1977, 1978. With regard to ideology, the argument hinges on a critique of the

concept of 'representation' and involves the assertion that signifying practices cannot be said to represent anything outside themselves. In my opinion, this rejection of representation is correct. But it does not follow that we can discover no pattern in the relations between classes and ideologies, or between classes and political organizations and struggles; nor that we cannot identify the mechanisms of selection and the limitations maintaining them. Hirst *et al.* offer their readers a choice between total class reductionism and total non-class reductionism (or class-independence) of ideology and politics — a choice which there is no reason to accept. 'The concept of "representation" entails the possibility that the "represented" determines its means of representation . . . If *any* autonomy is accorded to the action of the means, then the relation between them and their product cannot be given (this recalls the problems of the "relative autonomy" of political representation).' Hirst, *On Law and Ideology*, p. 71, emphasis added and original emphasis omitted.

22. For the trajectory of German liberal bourgeois opinion during the last third of the 19th century see E. Bramsted, *Aristocracy and the Middle Classes in Germany* (Chicago 1964) pp. 203ff.

23. If this is correct, then it would seem that Laclau's basic position on ideology in his very valuable work *Politics and Ideology* is untenable and inherently unstable. Laclau confronts us with the same choice between class and non-class reductionism as does Hirst: 'If we abandon the reductionist assumption that every ideological and political element has a necessary class-belonging and define classes as the poles of antagonistic production relations which have *no* necessary form of existence at the ideological and political levels. . .' (p. 160) emphasis added and original emphasis omitted. But then he continues: 'Let us assert, at the same time, the determination in the last instance of historical social processes by the relations of production, that is to say, by classes.' These two statements are linked by a conception of ideologies as an autonomous repertoire of interpellations which classes employ, combine or, as Laclau calls it, articulate in different ways in their struggle. The class character of an ideology lies in its 'articulating principle', which 'is always a class principle' (p. 164). But if classes have no necessary forms of ideological and political existence, if

ideologies and political forms have no necessary class character, how can we then identify the class character of the articulating principle? How can we know that it is *classes* which are forming and fighting states, combining and recombining ideologies, which are struggling for hegemony? How do we know that we are not just looking at class-independent states, parties, politicians and intellectuals? As far as I can see, there are only two coherent answers to these questions. *Either* the whole historical materialist problematic of determination by class and class struggle has to be abandoned — a path now being trodden by Hirst & Co. *Or* classes and the subjects of the class struggle must be conceived as being constituted by class-specific ideologies and forms of political practice. The general tenor of Laclau's book appears much closer to the second solution than to the first. Indeed, despite disclaimers to the contrary, the book contains formulations which, in a very vague and underdeveloped way, do point in the direction of a conception of class ideologies. The following is said, for instance, in a typical negative aside: 'These class ideological practices are determined not only by the insertion of a given class in the process of production. . .', and 'the ideology of a dominant class does not merely consist of a *Weltanschauung* which ideologically expresses its essence. . .' (p. 161). Well, 'not only' and 'not merely' is another way of saying 'also'.

24. O. Brunner, *Land und Herrschaft*, Brünn/München/Wien 1943; G. Duby, *Les trois ordres ou l'imaginaire du féodalisme*, Paris 1978; idem, *Guerriers et paysans*, Paris 1973; A. Joanna, *L'ordre social — mythes et hiérarchies dans la France du XVIe siècle*, Paris 1977; J. Foster, *Class Struggle and the Industrial Revolution*, London 1974; E. J. Hobsbawm, *Labouring Men*, London 1964; M. Perrot, *Les ouvriers en grève, France 1871-1890*, Paris 1974; E. P. Thompson, *The Making of the English Working Class*, London 1963; R. Trempe, *Les mineurs de Carmaux: 1848-1914* Paris 1971; M. Vester, *Die Entstehung des Proletariats als Lernprozess*, Frankfurt 1970; E. Genovese, *Roll Jordan Roll: The World the Slaves Made*, New York 1974.

25. G. Baglioni, *L'ideologia della borghesia industriale nell'Italia liberale*, Turin 1974; A. Hirschman, *The Passions and the Interests: Political Arguments for Capitalism Before its Triumph*, Princeton

132

1977; R. H. Tawney, *Religion and the Rise of Capitalism*, London 1922; M. Weber, *The Protestant Ethic and the Spirit of Capitalism*, New York 1930. The classical historical work on bourgeois ideology in France, B. Groethuysen, *Origines de l'esprit bourgeois en France*, Paris 1927, never went beyond the first volume, which dealt with Church doctrine in relation to the early development of capitalism under the *ancien regime*.

26. Concerning the working class among the most important studies are probably J. Goldthorpe, D. Lockwood *et al.*, *The Affluent Worker*, 3 vols., Cambridge 1968-69; and A. Touraine, *La conscience ouvriere*, Paris 1966. Two studies which I have found particularly fascinating are: M. Burawoy, *Manufacturing Consent*, Chicago 1979, and J. Martinez-Alier, *Labourers and Land-owners in Southern Spain*, London 1971. On the bourgeoisie there are: D. Baltzell, *Philadelphia Gentlemen*, Glencoe 1958; and F. Sutton, *The American Business Creed*, Cambridge, Mass., 1956. A very interesting research-project is being conducted by Bill Johnston, Michael Ornstein, Michael Stevenson and others at York University, Ontario. They are exploring how a great deal of ideological variation in survey material can be explained by Marxist conceptualizations of class (as developed by Carchedi, Poulantzas and Wright) as opposed to non-Marxist categories of region, occupation, education and income.

27. *Science, Class and Society*, pp. 375ff.

28. For another recent Marxist attempt at a theoretical determination of bourgeois ideology, see Labica, op. cit. The author singles out 'equality' as *the* crucial feature — which seems much too narrow to me.

29. Harriet Friedmann is one of the very few Marxists to have taken the concepts of petty-bourgeois and simple commodity production as objects for serious theoretical clarification and empirical investigation. See, for instance, her 'World Market, State and Family Farm: Bases of Household Production in the Era of Wage Labour', in *Comparative Studies in History and Society*, vol. 20, no. 4 (1978).

30. E. O. Wright, *Class Crisis and the State*, London, NLB, 1978.

31. Cf. R. Hilton, *Bondmen Made Free*, London 1978.

32. I presented an outline of such a theory to the 1979 Moscow

Congress of the International Political Science Association. The paper was entitled 'Enterprises, Markets and States. A First, Modest Contribution to a General Theory of Capitalist Politics'.

33. See my *Science, Class and Society*, pp. 326ff.
34. Gramsci, *Prison Notebooks*, London 1971.
35. Science, Class and Society, pp. 326ff.
36. Althusser, personal communication to the author, April 1979.
37. Poulantzas developed a similar argument in his last book.
38. R. Ebbinghausen, ed., *Bürgerlicher Staat und politische Legitimation*, Frankfurt 1976; J. Habermas, *Legitimationsprobleme im Spätkapitalismus*, Frankfurt 1973; N. Luhmann, *Legitimation durch Verfahren*, Neuwled 1969; J. O'Connor, *The Fiscal Crisis of the State*, New York 1973; C. Offe, *Strukturprobleme des kapitalistischen Staates*, Frankfurt 1973; A. Wolfe, *The Limits of Legitimacy*, New York 1977.
39. P. Bachrach, V. Baratz, *Power and Poverty*, New York 1970; R. Dahl, *Pluralist Democracy in the United States*, Chicago 1967; M. Mann, 'The Social Cohesion of Liberal Democracy', *American Sociological Review*, vol. XXXV (1970); *Pouvoirs*, no. 5, 1973.
40. M. Bulmer, ed., *Working-Class Images of Society*, London 1975; K. Kumar, 'Can Workers be Revolutionary?', *European Journal of Political Research*, vol. 6, no. 4 (1978); M. Mann, *Consciousness and Action among the Western Working Class*, London 1973; A. Wolpe, 'Some Problems Concerning Revolutionary Consciousness', *Socialist Register 1970*.
41. A subjectivist theory of history does not necessarily need to neglect the importance of unintended consequences. Jean-Paul Sartre's *Critique of Dialectical Reason*, London 1976, demonstrates this exceptional possibility amply and well.
42. For evidence see *Science, Class and Society*, pp. 297ff.
43. Cf. Theda Skocpol, *States and Social Revolutions*, Cambridge 1979; and for contrast, James Petras, 'Socialist Revolutions and Their Class Components', in *New Left Review*, no. 111 (1978). See also Barrington Moore's profound work, *Injustice: The Social Roots of Obedience and Revolt*, New York 1978.
44. See Alexander Rabinowitch's very thorough blow-by-blow study, *The Bolsheviks Come to Power*, London, NLB, 1979.

Printed in the United States
by Baker & Taylor Publisher Services